Scenes with My Son

Scenes with My Son

Love and Grief in the Wake of Suicide

———

Robert Hubbard

WILLIAM B. EERDMANS PUBLISHING COMPANY
GRAND RAPIDS, MICHIGAN

Wm. B. Eerdmans Publishing Co.
4035 Park East Court SE, Grand Rapids, Michigan 49546
www.eerdmans.com

Book design by Lydia Hall

Printed in the United States of America

29 28 27 26 25 24 23   1 2 3 4 5 6 7

ISBN 978-0-8028-8344-5

Library of Congress Cataloging-in-Publication Data

A catalog record for this book is available from the Library of
Congress.

A version of "On ECT and Rainbows" was originally printed in the
Northwestern Review 5, issue 1 (2020).

A version of "In Gratitude for a Son: Stumbling through the ACTS
Prayer" was originally published in the *Reformed Journal* blog on December 22, 2020, and is reprinted with permission.

"April and the *Mare of Easttown*" was originally published under the
title "Anger in Easttown" in *Think Christian* on May 26, 2021. It is
reprinted here with the permission of Jonathan Larsen, TC editor.

For Auggie

Contents

Or what strong hand can hold his [Time's] swift foot back?
Or who his spoil of beauty can forbid?
O, none, unless this miracle have might,
That in black ink my love may still shine bright.

SHAKESPEARE, SONNET 65

Foreword

For a parent to experience the death of a child is terrible. One is assaulted by grief: grief over the loss of the one loved, of course, but also grief over the assault to oneself. One's hopes for one's child have been ripped out, one's plans, one's aspirations, one's apprehensions. Where those once were there is now only a gaping wound in oneself.

For a parent to undergo the death of a child *by suicide* is beyond terrible. Intertwined with grief there are now self-lacerating feelings of guilt and failure. "If only I had done this." "If only I had done that." "If only I had noticed that other thing." One finds oneself helpless in the face of one's child's depression; nonetheless, the "if onlys" keep coming.

Robert Hubbard's *Scenes with My Son: Love and Grief in the Wake of Suicide* is the gripping and harrowing story of the life of the author's son, Auggie, who, after years of suffering from depression, lost his life to suicide in his late teens. The book consists of brief vignettes, vividly written, story seamlessly blended with reflection. Hubbard has an extraordinary gift for noticing the telling detail, and he is amazingly candid and forthcoming in exposing his heart and soul to the reader. The story is sometimes raw; every now and then I had to put it down for a while. The vignettes are organized into three acts: "Beautiful Boy," "The Family Monster" (depression), and "The Life After."

Gerard Manley Hopkins introduced the word "inscape" into the English language. It was his translation of a word that he found in the medieval philosopher Duns Scotus: *haecceitas*, literally, *thisness*. It was Hopkins's idea that everything has a distinctive inscape, a distinctive thisness—the inscape of some things more distinctive than that of others. Auggie, on his father's telling, had an inscape like none other. Never, says the father, has he met anyone like him. Neither have I, judging from Hubbard's description. What stands out is Auggie's intensity: the intensity of his joys, the intensity of his rages, of his intellectual interests, of his depression, of his love for animals—on and on, intensity.

Corresponding to Auggie's intensity is the intensity of his father's love, a love that shines out from every page. *Scenes with My Son* is a love story, the story of a father's devoted love for his gifted, troubled son. It was a love that was lived every day on the edge: Would Auggie do something self-destructive today? The story is rich in detail, but never voyeuristic. Hubbard tells us when and where he found his dead son; he does not describe what he saw, nor how his son took his life.

Those who have experienced the death of a child by suicide will experience a spiritual and emotional balm in finding a soulmate who shares their kind of grief and guilt. Those who live with a child struggling with depression will likewise experience the balm of solidarity. And for the rest of us: we will be inspired by the example of a young life of boundless intensity and by the example of a father's love that matched that intensity.

NICHOLAS WOLTERSTORFF
Noah Porter Professor Emeritus of Philosophical Theology,
Yale University
Senior Research Fellow, Institute for Advanced Studies in Culture,
University of Virginia

Prologue

I never thought I would be able to write this book.

On October 23, 2020, our youngest son, August Robert Hubbard, Auggie to me, died by suicide. He was nineteen years old. After a tenacious, nearly five-year battle, depression took his life.

A couple of months after that terrible day, a family member told me, "You need to write about Auggie, Bob."

The idea made me sick to my stomach.

True, in the days and weeks that followed Auggie's death, I managed to compose some brief updates for friends and family on social media. But these relatively short summaries were a steaming pile of hell to write. I only sent them out into the ether so that our concerned community would have some idea of what had happened to the Hubbard clan. After the funeral, April and I went off the social grid, escaping to her family farm in rural North Dakota; people were asking about us.

Also true, over the span of two decades, I have written three different full-length, autobiographical, one-person shows that I performed at fringe festivals, churches, and community centers. The stories that made up these scripts included personal tales ranging from growing up with an alcoholic father to giving up on atheism in favor of Christianity. But my modest history of trying to turn difficult experiences into art failed to convince me that

I could ever write about Auggie. If memories of him caused me to break down multiple times each day, how in God's name could I survive writing about our beautiful boy? No way.

A few months later, I walked into the friendly neighborhood coffee shop where I often hide out for hours grading, writing, or prepping for class. I ordered my obligatory Americano and claimed my usual table nearest the back wall of the shop. As I marshaled the will to grade a week's worth of accumulated journal entries for a theatre course, I noticed an old acquaintance cautiously walk toward me. We attended the same church a long time ago. Since he lives in a nearby town, I rarely see him around. As he approached my table, I struggled to recall his name. I also braced myself for the inevitable awkward condolences sure to come. I learned through repetition that the first encounter with someone since we lost our child usually includes a painful and awkward exchange. They say something like, "I cannot imagine what you are going through" or "There are no words." Both clichés are completely true, of course, and come from only the best intentions. In receiving them, I try to express the requisite gratitude but also guard my heart against the simmering rush of grief that may explosively transform into tears at any moment.

"Hi, Bob," he said, leaning over my table.

"Hi there, buddy," I replied, still waiting for his name to pop into my head.

"I wanted to let you know that you and your family are in our prayers. We were so sorry to hear about Auggie. There are no words . . ."

Nodding my head, I responded with my pat yet sincere reply while simultaneously choking back the massive lump forming in my throat: "I appreciate that. Thank you. We need your prayers."

He continued, "I also wanted to say that I have read and reread your social media posts about Auggie. I look at them often."

"Ah, thank you." And then I couldn't help but ask: "Why?" Again. I barely know this fellow. He barely knows me or my family.

Then, his voice suddenly cracking, this man whose name I could not remember shared with me a staggeringly terrible circumstance involving one of his children. When he finished, I had no idea what to say. The vulnerable and awkward moment lingered as I resisted the impulse to fill the silence with *there are no words.*

After a deep breath, my old acquaintance concluded, "Reading about your struggles and your love for your son helps me get through this time. I just needed to tell you that."

After more silence followed by mutual knowing nods and affirmations, he left me to my grading. The thought crossed my mind at the time that maybe I should try to write more about Auggie.

A second encounter that made me consider writing this book took place later that same summer. My wife, April, is a talented theatre artist who holds her master of fine arts in directing. The year before COVID shut all theatre down, she found a wonderful gig directing for a summer stock theatre in North Dakota, her home state. When the theatre finally reopened, she decided to turn down their newest offer to direct because doing so would mean more time apart from me; we lost so much the past year; we needed time together. Wanting to spend as many hours as possible with April but also knowing how much this directing job meant to her, I proposed a crazy solution. What if I stayed with her in North Dakota while she directed her play? This decision meant me illegally squatting in a women's dormitory for three weeks. The minor crime seemed reasonable under the circumstances. While April directed, I passed the hours swimming laps at the local YMCA and hanging out in coffee shops in the postboom (yet still surprisingly vibrant) fracking town near the Canadian border. During this time, I also read a beautiful novel called *Hamnet.*[1]

My love for reading novels had become a casualty of grief. For months after losing our boy, I periodically tried to read. After lifelessly scanning the same paragraph multiple times, I always gave up. The ravages of situational depression prevented my addled brain from concentrating long enough to comprehend extended passages of the written word. In the hopes that this affliction might pass, I picked up a copy of Maggie O'Farrell's *Hamnet* at a local North Dakota bookstore. This acclaimed feminist novel fictionalizes the story of the courtship and marriage between Anne Hathaway and a young Stratford lad only described in the book as "the Latin teacher" or, later, the "writer." As implied by the title, a large portion of the biographical fiction focuses on the death of their son, Hamnet. I doubted that I would be able to read O'Farrell's delicate and enthralling novel. Fortunately, my slowly healing brain finally cooperated. Some of the passages about the Shakespeares' loss of their precocious child predictably tore me to tatters, but I pressed on. For the first time in eight long months, I read a novel from cover to cover.

The title of O'Farrell's novel shares a name, sort of, with Shakespeare's most acclaimed tragic hero. Since regularized English spelling did not yet exist, Hamnet and Hamlet were essentially the same name within their original Elizabethan context. Near the end of the novel, "the writer," now separated from his Stratford family to run his successful theatre company in London, pens his most famous play. Depicting an act of redemptive grieving, O'Farrell spins the story of a father artfully infusing the rich personality of his deceased son into the avatar of a Danish prince. By showing the public what G. K. Chesterton called Hamlet's "great soul,"[2] William Shakespeare honors his deceased son. He also gifts the world with a timeless work of art. O'Farrell wrote fiction, not history, but her premise must contain some truth. Shortly after a profound personal loss, the real William Shakespeare did indeed name one of his greatest artistic creations after his deceased son.

This book in no appreciable way resembles *Hamlet*, nor I, Shakespeare; such comparisons are laughable. Nonetheless, the climax of *Hamnet* inspired me to write this little book. Like O'Farrell's fictional Shakespeare, I love the idea of using whatever limited abilities I may hold as a writer to let the world know about Auggie's great soul.

Writers and artists often talk about visits from "the muse." As a Christian, I believe the muse to be synonymous with the Holy Spirit, who sometimes whispers in our ear. I finished reading *Hamnet* while sitting at a North Dakota coffee shop in early July. And as soon as I closed the cover, dozens of vignettes and stories connected to Auggie's short life flooded my brain. I grabbed my notebook and wrote them down. Twenty minutes later, my pen strokes blurry with tears, I found myself staring at the outline for a book in three parts—three acts, if you will.

In the first definitive book on drama in the Western tradition, *The Poetics*, Aristotle observes that, unlike the Homeric odes, drama's uniqueness comes from being "in the form of action, not narrative."[3] For an ephemeral art form that lives in the moment, theatre relies on the present tense to lend a sense of immediacy to the telling. And like theatre, I try to place the reader in each moment. While time lines and topics often overlap between the chapters, you can think of each one like a short play riffing on self-contained memories. In a way, the stories function like a collection of linked dramatic monologues.

I never planned to write this book until I wrote it. I never thought I could, but it turns out I had to. For Auggie, and hopefully, for others.

ACT I

Beautiful Boy

The First Christmas

Today, December 21, 2000, the jet-stream-driven snow-belt of West Michigan earns its reputation for spectacle. Large, wet flakes fall from the sky in a heavy frenzy of white that suspends the normal activities of life. Everyone hunkers down; snowplows can't compete; signs and stoplights are unreadable. The city of Grand Rapids, Michigan, resembles a winter movie set where the art director got carried away. A hell of a day to have a baby, but what are you going to do?

Our first two boys beat their due dates, barely, but boy number three has other plans. He blew by his projected arrival, stubbornly claiming more territory inside his mother—more ounces by the day. The doctor finally decided to induce labor on December 21, 2000. But a full day's regimen of oxytocin produces nothing but anxiety. At 6 p.m., we make the decision to suspend April's treatment and try to induce again tomorrow morning.

During those hours waiting for the meds to kick in, we nervously watched through the hospital window as this winter solstice blizzard covered Grand Rapids in slippery snow. Now, after eight unproductive hours in the birthing room, I have to make a risky decision. Should I or should I not attempt to go back to our house to save our dog's life?

I thought I'd taken care of everything: bag packed (check); gas in the car (check); child care (check)—safe from the storm, our three-year-old and two-year-old are currently enjoying a sleepover at a generous friend's home. But our dog! When the decision to induce was made, I assumed that this whole thing would be wrapped up by noon. And I never thought to check the weather report. With each new inch of fresh snow, I freshly regretted leaving our border collie baby in our fenced backyard before we drove to the hospital that morning.

"Nothing's going to happen tonight, it seems pretty clear," I finally say to April. "I think I need to go home and make sure our dog is still alive."

"Yes. Take care of him. But you had better get back here quickly if things start moving."

"I promise, I will."

With the roads such a mess, I consider walking, but I didn't wear the proper shoes for such a slushy hike. I'm not sure how our low-slung Saturn hatchback, our first big purchase as a married couple, keeps its momentum through unplowed streets knee-deep in snow, but it does. I successfully drive the mile and a half from the hospital to our snowbound house in southeast Grand Rapids. Parking in the buried driveway is impossible, so I abandon the car near the side of the road, hoping some unsuspecting driver will not plow into it in the middle of the night. With relief, I find our timid, anxious dog cowering under our little deck in our little back yard contemplating his dramatically diminished status in our family unit. A call to the hospital assures me that nothing is likely to happen tonight, so I collapse into a restless sleep.

—

The sun and I rise simultaneously the next morning, and the world has become a magical white accentuated by a piercingly bright blue sky—the thick blanket of snow making a symbolic sculpture garden of parked pickups and stop signs and mailboxes. It takes me almost forty minutes to dig out the car from the five-foot wall of snow the snowplow left behind, but I'm grateful the plow didn't hit the car or have it towed away. The world feels as fresh as a newborn, and I take the snow as a good omen. I leave the dog some food and get my ass to the hospital. I have a son to meet.

But not yet. The long labor continues and is tough on April. Our boy clearly wants to come out, but his enormous Hubbard head, my inheritance I'm afraid, slows his exit. In late afternoon I notice the doctor move to the rear of the room to consult with her nurse. Under her breath, I hear, "prep for cesarean." As if in response, our rebellious child bears down. Ten minutes later, he finally makes his appearance in the world: over ten pounds of gorgeous, tuckered-out humanity. Huge blue eyes peer at us through his enormous, oddly shaped head. Just a wisp of blond hair. Glory.

Since we learned the due date, we knew that Christmastime would never again be the same. Just three days before billions celebrate the birth of a Lord and Savior, we celebrate our own small miracle of incarnation, the birth of August Robert Hubbard.

This is the best Christmas ever.

Day-Care Romeo

The large window overlooking the toddlers' room is decorated with the imaginative creations of artists who still poop in their pants. Even through the canopy of squiggly stick-figures and drawings of massive flowers, I still manage to catch his eyes after only a few seconds of voyeuristic playtime observation. Through the glass, I see Auggie shout, "Daddy" in a wide-eyed, full-bodied, jubilant giggle.

The decision to move to Iowa made day care a necessity. April and I both recently started full-time teaching gigs as theatre professors at two nearby colleges, and our three rambunctious boys were all still under the age of four. Fortunately, the flexibility of our jobs permits us to carefully engineer our schedules to get as much time with our boys as possible. Most days I get to work before 7 a.m. so that I can pick the boys up by 3 p.m. April drops them off by 10 a.m. and stays at work until 6 p.m. And although the financial cost is substantial, the day care we selected seems like Club Med compared to the Colorado high plains trailer parks where I grew up. For five hours a day, our kids enjoy nutritional food, board games, excellent toys, an abundance of high-quality socialization, and, of course, arts and crafts.

Admittedly, the fact that I am the one who usually picks the kids up from day care rather than drops them off probably further skews my positive perceptions. April's more difficult task of locating three matching pairs of shoes each morning requires a PhD in patience. And forget about matching pairs of gloves and boots once winter sets in. But my positive feelings about this day care are not just a function of my own history or the easier logistics of my daily assignment. I also get to watch Auggie say good-bye to his caregivers each afternoon.

Auggie's brothers seem to do just fine in their respective rooms. Charlie finds a teacher who will play board games with him for most of the day, so he's in heaven. George usually prefers to sit by himself under a play structure and daydream complicated adventures; we call these destinations "George world." Auggie, not yet two years old, spends his late mornings and early afternoons wooing women.

Each afternoon, I get to peer through the window covered with primitive toddler drawings until Auggie's huge blue eyes twinkle at me in recognition. But before he comes to me, before I lift his little body into my arms and hug the giggles out of him, before we put on his shoes and coat, before *all* the precious rituals of daily reunion, Auggie must first properly say good-bye. He bolts to both kindly caregivers who staff his room. When he reaches them, he throws his arms skyward and offers a sweet, earnest hug. When his caregivers kneel to meet his daily embrace, Auggie sinks his head onto their shoulders and squeezes with gusto.

As he hugs, his eyes crunch closed with passionate determination and sincerity. He seems so much in love with them, with everyone, with day care, with life.

Turning Blue with Rage
(with Some Forced Allusions to Aristotle and "Dover Beach")

From nearly the first day August Robert Hubbard entered the world until now, I have never met anyone who enjoys himself so much. As he approaches two years old, Auggie brims with happiness, excitement, and delight. The surprise of an ice-cream sandwich, being included in his brothers' games, a zerbert blown onto his chubby tummy—all these magical events deliver Auggie into sustained bouts of ecstatic joy. Our bouncy boy is a gift to be around, so jubilant, so cheerful, so new.

It's also the case that in rare moments Auggie turns mad as hell. These flashes of rage usually occur when he physically hurts himself or when he believes himself the victim of a great injustice. He may stub his bare toe on a misplaced rock in the backyard or bump his head on the coffee table's evil corner. Or worse, he may receive clandestine intelligence regarding a piece of candy that one of his brothers received, or a negligent parent might prematurely turn off an episode of *Teletubbies*. In these moments, God help us; Auggie turns blue with rage.

Auggie *literally* turns blue with rage.

Here is how it works. Immediately after enduring a physical injury or a perceived inequality, Auggie initially appears strangely tranquil. To an untrained eye, he is fine. Careful observation reveals, however, the invasion of barely perceptible tremors vibrating his otherwise frozen little body. Astute viewers may also notice that no breath enters or escapes his mouth, so complete and consuming is the escalating rage.

Next comes the color change. His face takes on a fiery glow as the capillary loops within his huge cheeks flush crimson. Then the hue of his skin metamorphoses two steps along the color wheel from fire engine red to a pale blue. During this transformation, Auggie's angry mouth may open into a contorted snarl, although no air yet escapes his petrified scowl. The color conversion takes several seconds and is quite jarring. Just at the point when the transition from red to blue concludes, he faints. His unconscious little body flops onto the ground like a top-heavy Jenga tower. When he wakes up a few seconds later, oh my. Confused and furious to find himself on the floor, he screams bloody murder with enough volume to rattle nearby windows.

Sometimes when he faints, Auggie hits his huge head. After a necessary gulp of oxygen, this added indignity causes the entire episode to begin again. As students of this unique physiological response, April and I become practitioners at minimizing the damage. Before our enflamed son turns blue, we whisk him into our arms or lay him gently on the floor. "You are okay. Breathe," we repeat. But despite our assurances and coaching, his rage response never shortens. The cycle is involuntary: silent outrage, turning red, turning blue, passing out. Every. Single. Time. Once, an understandably freaked-out babysitter whom we forgot to warn about her charge's unique condition got as far as talking with a 911 operator before being interrupted by Auggie's inevitable inhalation followed by livid wails.

—

Our son's deep capacity for joy and rage epitomized his unique personality. The ancient Aegean adage "moderation in all things" did not apply to Auggie. He was all-in; involuntary passions and impulses ruled him. From infancy to the dawn of adolescence, he

lived mostly in a state of joy. He embodied the gift of joy. He occasionally experienced waves of rage, but, overall, the tide of Auggie's
optimistic nature lifted all nearby boats. Indeed, the world seemed
to lie before preadolescent Auggie like a land of dreams, so various,
so beautiful, so new.

The moments of blue rage seemed to his family like a colorful
eccentricity. We did not know then that these extreme shifts in
mood hinted at dangerous imbalances to come, a portent of the
darkling plain from which there was no escape nor help for pain.

Story out of Head

All our boys loved to read, but Auggie was the most susceptible to the transporting power of story. When April read to all three boys at bedtime, toddler Auggie eagerly entered into fiction intended for older children. In the company of his older brothers, he listened to the works of C. S. Lewis, Katherine Paterson, J. K. Rowling, and others. As April read these stories, Auggie situated his little body as close to her as humanly possible and tightly fixed his huge blue eyes upon his mother's lips, as if the words transformed into images on her breath. A funny piece of fiction prompted convulsions of laughter that he could not control, especially if it involved bodily functions. An unfair plot twist that threatened the happiness of a beloved protagonist threw him into despair. And if the story was exciting, well, forget about sleep for a while.

When my turn came to lead story time, I imitated a family tradition we called "story out of head." This long-form improvisation was started by a creative grandfather during sleepover visits that often included three rambunctious cousins in addition to our three boys. The tradition involved asking each child to contribute a character that their grandpa George then wove into an epic tale of adventure and morality. In my less ambitious adaptation, the characters became fixed over time, one representing each boy. Our oldest son's favorite amphibian stuffed animal inspired "Charlie the

Frog"; "George the Monkey" derived from our middle son's affection for his namesake book series, Curious George. Auggie's character became "Auggie the Octopus," after the intelligent sea creature that his day-care teachers used to decorate his name tag.

For thirty minutes or more every other evening, I spun my yarns. On a good night, I could make Auggie shake with delight when his octopus conspicuously farted in a library or hurtled into outer space on a homemade rocket or went back in time to the Middle Ages to fight the Black Knight. Despite his glee, Auggie could also be discerning. When I could no longer think of original plots, I sometimes plopped the namesake characters into the plays of Shakespeare or the epic tales of Homer. One night, Charlie the Frog, George the Monkey, and Auggie the Octopus hid inside a giant wooden horse so that they could finally conquer their rivals, the Trojans. Midway through the surprise attack, three-year-old Auggie interrupted the tale to admonish me: "Daddy, that doesn't sound like your story. You didn't make that up."

When Auggie learned to read for himself, he dove deeper into the world of fiction. Like the other obsessions that came throughout his life, reading took complete control. The reading obsession hit a high mark in fifth grade when Auggie fixated on a program called Accelerated Reader. After reading an approved book, elementary school students could take a comprehension quiz on a computer at the school library. If they passed, they earned points that a savvy librarian visualized as cumulative scores on a graph posted on a bulletin board for all the school to see. That was all the motivation Auggie needed.

For most of his fifth-grade year, he devoured books and posted points at a remarkable rate. Like many in his generation, he seemed predisposed to dystopian young adult fiction. Auggie vanished into books with titles like *The Hunger Games, Divergent, Maze Runner, The Sin Eater, Aragon, The Giver, Enders Game,* and *Ready Player One.* One evening late in May near the end of his fifth-grade year, we got him to take a break from reading long enough to eat dinner with us. During the meal, he reported that he and an equally reading-obsessed rival classmate had both shattered the Accelerated Reader record for their school. Auggie was slightly ahead, he said, but his determined classmate, the son of a local physician, was only a few points behind him. With just five days left until the end of the contest, extreme measures must be taken.

Desperate to win, Auggie unveiled the book that would put him out of reach. From his school backpack, he pulled out a thick, unabridged copy of Victor Hugo's *Les Misérables*. "I looked it up," he said. "It's worth a lot of points!" The only book Auggie could find worth more in the Accelerated Reader program was Margaret Mitchell's *Gone with the Wind*. He also had a copy of Mitchell's problematic piece of Southern fiction lodged in his overstuffed backpack. But based on the descriptions, Auggie preferred to tackle *Les Misérables*. April and I gently wondered aloud if it was a good idea to read a book so far above his grade level. With wild-eyed confidence, Auggie replied, "But I get 105 points for it. Can you imagine, 105 points!"

Later that week, his rival passed him in total points, logging two more books to his cumulative total. Trailing behind, Auggie dug deeper into his secret-weapon classic, but the going was understandably tough. One night that week, I heard him in his room reading Hugo's long, descriptive passages out loud to better understand the nineteenth-century prose. The Thursday night before the final day that students could take an Accelerated Reader quiz, Auggie still had a third of the book to go; he stayed up for hours trying to finish all 1,462 pages of *Les Misérables*. By the morning, he claimed that his eleven-year-old eyes had passed over every page of Hugo's masterpiece.

Unfortunately, when Auggie took the comprehension quiz later that day, he failed to get enough questions right to pass. His all-consuming, herculean effort yielded zero points. Although they both set new school records, Auggie came in second place to his rival. His Accelerated Reader career ended in what was, for him, failure. He stopped all leisure reading for a time and would not speak about his love of books for months.

—

Although Auggie's passion for reading in the years to come occasionally went dormant, it always forcefully returned. In middle school he consumed classical fantasy, starting with *The Hobbit* and then quickly finishing all three *Lord of the Rings* novels. With Tolkien as his gateway drug, high school Auggie dove deeply into the violent, sexy realm of *Game of Thrones*. Then his mom introduced him to adult science fiction, and off they went. Together they dove into massive series like *The Expanse*, *Old Man's War*, and *Red Rising*. Other stand-alone sci-fi favorites included *Beacon 23* and *The Martian*; the latter begins with swearing, and April remembers hearing Auggie giggle as soon as he started reading it.

His brother George got Auggie into Kurt Vonnegut, as they both devoured *Slaughterhouse Five* and *Breakfast of Champions*. No doubt there was a time when Auggie could have taught a graduate seminar on the works of Neil Gaiman. During what was supposed to be his junior year of high school, our then-depression-stricken son endured his longest hospital stay of forty days of in-patient care. Before our daily visits to see him, April and I picked up reading reinforcements at the Sioux Falls Barnes and Noble. Our stack included Gaiman's *Neverwhere*, *Good Omens*, *Norse Mythology*, *Odd and the Frost Giant*, *Stardust*, and of course, *American Gods*. Among the books I recommended to him over the years, Auggie particularly appreciated *The Catcher in the Rye*, *The Sun Also Rises*, and *The Autobiography of Malcolm X*. Each new discovery prompted lengthy descriptive summaries and extended conversations full of hyperbolic pronouncements that this was the best book he ever read!

For Auggie, books served as a form of comfort, a tool of enlightenment, and a surefire way to change the world.

The Jedi of Windmill Park

The *Star Wars* phenomenon strikes four-year-old Auggie with the force of an exploding Imperial Death Star. Of course, George Lucas's fictional universe captured the imaginations of billions of fans over multiple generations. Among his peers, however, Auggie's passionate dedication stands out.

His status as the youngest child in the family likely fast-tracked Auggie's obsessive love for all things *Star Wars*. As parents, we mostly succeeded in making his older brothers wait to see the iconic films until they reached an appropriate age. But how, in decency and fairness, can we allow siblings to see much-anticipated *Star Wars* prequels but leave out a desperate, pleading, shockingly persuasive four-year-old little brother? We try but miserably fail to keep the *Star Wars* genie in the age-appropriate bottle. By the time the third prequel, *Revenge of the Sith*, arrives in theaters, all three sons have watched the existing *Star Wars* canon multiple times on DVD from the shelter of our basement rec room. April and I consider not allowing Auggie to attend the PG-13 premiere in the movie theater, but we again succumb to our kindergartner's power of persuasion. How can we possibly leave our passionate child with a babysitter while the rest of the family hedonistically enjoys popcorn and an exploding volcano planet? To make ourselves feel better, we settle on the questionable parenting strategy of sitting beside Auggie in the theater with the intent of covering his wide eyes as soon as light sabers start severing limbs. Auggie is thrilled to be included.

As a result of this early overexposure, Luke, Leia, Darth Maul, Darth Vader, Anakin, and Obi Wan all make deep impressions on Auggie's developing personal ethic. Since DVDs of the prequels introduced Generation Z to Star Wars, our youngest Jedi lover sadly suffers from an affliction common among his misguided generation: a lack of artistic discernment. My attempts to mentor our young Padawan toward the bright side of the Force fail as Auggie resolutely and blasphemously believes that Jar Jar Binks is indeed an excellent character and that *Attack of the Clones* will one day be regarded as a better film than *The Empire Strikes Back*. Despite grievous errors in judgment, April and I ultimately approve of the *Star Wars* influencer who latches the most firmly onto Auggie's heart. More than Anakin, Luke, or Han, Auggie loves Yoda. For years, this wise and tiny green Jedi master reaches from his swamp planet home of Dagobah across galaxies and time into the imagination of an infatuated little kid in Iowa. In matters of greatest importance, Yoda serves as Auggie's go-to teacher, hero, and guide.

"Strap me in my car seat, you must," giggles Auggie as I help secure him in his seat for a drive.

When Halloween rolls around, Auggie of course demands to go as Yoda. April resourcefully locates a perfect facsimile of a Yoda robe from her college's theater costume shop. In a stroke of costuming genius, she squeezes Auggie's head into the legging from a green pair of pantyhose; this trick contorts Auggie's face to evoke Yoda's wrinkly mug. The women's dorms at the college where I teach traditionally host a Halloween party for the public, generously handing out candy to the costumed masses. Dressed in eclectic get-ups also borrowed from the college's costume shop, George and Charlie lead the way as we trick-or-treat down the crowded, narrow hallways of Fern Smith Hall. Amid the chaotic throng of sugar-charged children, April and I take turns holding our young Jedi in our arms above the bustling fray. As the good-natured college students place candy in our children's repurposed ice-cream buckets, Auggie theatrically contorts and twists his hands toward the candy-givers as if manipulating them with the Force.

"Give me the Hershey bar, you must," he commands with an exultant, twisted grin.

In many ways, Yoda makes an ideal hero for Auggie. As the youngest of three brothers, he intimately identifies with the perils of being the smallest Jedi in the house. Like all siblings, his generally good-natured big brothers still tease and push the youngest member of the family around, a condition made worse by Auggie's innate oppositional nature. So, when he watches Yoda miraculously drop his arthritic posture and effortlessly summersault into action to battle Count Dooku with his signature green lightsaber in hand, well, Auggie sees his soul mate. Yes, Yoda is inherently small, and kind, and wise, but he still knows how to use the Force to righteously kick some butt when absolutely necessary; he takes oppressors down.

For two straight years from ages four to five, Auggie only requests one birthday or Christmas present. Whether asked by parents, grandparents, aunts, or uncles, his reprise remains the same: "Please give me a lightsaber." Relatives comply, and by Christmas of 2005 Auggie proudly owns nine different lightsabers. Some are the cheap, low-grade plastic knockoffs that expand like accordions when waved with force. These are fine for battles with his brothers in the basement. The most-prized members of his collection, the ones that carry substantial weight and craftsmanship, impressively light up and magically replicate the trademarked humming sound when wielded through the air.

For a joyful boy with more than his share of delightful eccentricities, one charming behavior stands out. In the early spring of 2006, Auggie adopts the almost daily practice of taking one of his precious, high-end lightsabers to Windmill Park across the street from our house. Whether by himself or surrounded by other playing children he ignores, he establishes a territory in an open space somewhere between the merry-go-round and the jungle gym. Once in place, he dramatically extends his lightsaber to its full and proper length. With the precision of a martial artist, he then practices his Jedi moves, making of them a solo dance routine. In long phrases of saber fencing, he thrusts and cuts, and blocks, the complicated choreography inspired by the lightsaber battles in the films that Auggie has so carefully studied. Only he can see the imaginary aggressors with whom he spars. Like a medieval shadow boxer, our six-year-old boy weaves his way through the public park with a glowing saber in hand. A devoted Padawan to the great Yoda, Auggie understands that he must properly train to be truly great; he's putting in the time.

But life can be cruel to creative dreamers who do not follow society's norms.

For one local bully, the repeated image of Auggie joyfully playing by himself with his lightsaber in the park is too much to tolerate. This interloper with clear impulse-control issues has already earned a reputation for pushing kids around. Sitting with our dog on a bench some thirty yards away, I do not hear his exact words when he approaches Auggie, but he apparently challenges my son to a lightsaber duel. With the confidence of a skilled Jedi warrior who has properly prepared, Auggie picks up the gauntlet.

Before I realize what is happening, the bully grabs a large stick from the ground and the two boys face off. Within a second, the much bigger challenger swings his block of wood at Auggie's waiting lightsaber. Of course, the stick knocks the plastic toy from Auggie's surprised hands. It falls onto the ground with a chunk of hard plastic missing. From my distanced spot, I stand up and yell, "Hey, that's enough." But before I can get to the other side of the park, the bully picks up the cracked lightsaber and repeatedly strikes Auggie with it. When I reach the fray, my shocked son is curled up on the ground. I wrench the lightsaber from the aggressor's hands and somehow resist the primal urge to punch the little shit's lights out.

Instead, I shout, "Leave him alone."

Like most true bullies, the boy immediately cowers. First, he tries to shake it off, saying, "Hey, we were only playing." Then he recognizes me as a coworker of his parents and immediately begs, "Please don't tell my mom about this."

I couldn't care less about this aggressive child's request. "Just leave," I say and turn my attention to my physically fine but shattered little boy.

—

I hate the lessons Auggie learned in the park that day. I hate that he found out that, no matter how much he practices, a plastic lightsaber will never protect him against a bully with a big stick. I hate that he lost his innocence. I hate that, on this spring day in Windmill Park, the Force was nowhere to be found. Most of all, I hate that from that day forward, the Jedi of Windmill Park was never seen again.

Official NFL-Sized Football

I don't want a stupid, little kid's football. I want the same one that Brandon Marshall catches," proclaims nine-year-old Auggie as we inspect the aisle of footballs at the Sioux City Scheels. Our family has driven forty-five miles and braved the early holiday crowds to visit the nearest real shopping mall. The list of things to do today includes scouting possible presents for upcoming birthday and Christmas celebrations.

"Don't you think it would be smarter to get a football closer to the size of the ones you will actually use if you play in high school?"

"No! I don't want a toy. I want the real thing. I want the official NFL-sized football!"

At nearly $100 a pop, the "real thing" means that Auggie will receive only one Christmas present from his parents this year. But he will be delighted with his 28½-inch long circumference, 21¼-inch short circumference, regulation leather, Wilson football. Against my advice, he will overinflate the ball just a bit because he believes this makes it easier to catch. The minor enhancement will make the already substantial football appear even larger. But maybe he is right. Auggie inherited his Grandpa Blomquist's massive hands. Even though he is only in the fourth grade, the NFL regulation ball looks at home in his huge, impressive grip, which was a good thing because he will carry it everywhere.

I mean everywhere.

Auggie will beg his fourth-grade teacher to let him clutch his Christmas present through math and social studies lessons; he will pledge never to throw it or ever let it even touch the floor while he holds it at his desk. He will take his leather appendage through the lunch line, I will be told, which will make balancing his tray with only one free hand precarious. At recess, Auggie will demand that the daily pickup touch-football scrimmage exclusively be played with his regulation ball instead of the easier-to-throw toys that the school provided. Most days, the older kids he plays with will oblige. One day his brother George will share some elementary school gossip with me: "Dad, a kid at school told me that he saw Auggie kissing his football in the library." I will not doubt it.

Then, after months of constant daily contact, the treasured football will vanish; we will never learn what happened. I suspect that our single-minded and forgetful son accidentally left his Christmas present somewhere it should not have been, maybe in a public restroom, on a bus, or in the swimming-pool locker room. My suspicion will come from experience since I possess the same forgetful gene. In fear of our family's scatterbrained proclivity, I will write HUBBARD with a black Sharpie in three different places on the prized football. My dad did the same thing for me on an expensive baseball mitt in deference to *my* absent-minded nature. In our fishbowl town where everyone seems to know who we are, I will be surprised that no one ever returns Auggie's expensive treasure. He will try to be stoic about the loss, but we will be able to tell that he is devastated. He will always have a difficult time caring for the material things he loves the most.

Although Auggie will make do with lesser footballs for a time, his obsession with the sport will comically rage on. I successfully pass down my irrational love for the Denver Broncos to all three of my sons. Although they initially comply, Charlie and George will eventually outgrow my silly fixation on a team of strange men who live in Denver. Auggie, on the other hand, will scream in joy and wail in agony with me while we watch the games. He collects dozens of worthless Denver Broncos football cards, stored under plastic in a binder in his room. He loves to regale listeners with Broncos trivia whether they ask or not. He will be able to name every starting offensive lineman from the 1978 Super Bowl team. He methodically rewatches a DVD commemorating John Elway's first Super Bowl victory, especially the aging quarterback's iconic helicopter lunge. When my sister's older children included the Hubbard men in their Fantasy Football league, Auggie made dozens of lineup changes every week and relentlessly begged his cousins and brothers to trade him their best players.

I almost regret passing down my football fanaticism. During Christmas break of 2009, our family watched a pivotal Broncos game on TV while spending the holidays at April's family farm in North Dakota. Auggie became so inconsolable after the Philadelphia Eagles abruptly ended the Broncos' playoff hopes that he couldn't eat the Christmas supper that his grandma Violet lovingly prepared. Conversely, few euphoric highs compare to the rocking joy our family shared when Tim Tebow threw his miracle overtime touchdown pass to beat the Pittsburgh Steelers in the 2011 wild card playoff game. The glory of that day!

But for me, the most football fun of all took place in the public park across the street from our home. Growing up, all three boys and I lived our evenings in this block-long tulip-filled green space dotted with playground equipment and miniature windmills. We must have played ten thousand hours of touch football on the stretch of green between the farmers' market and the band shell. Most of the time, Auggie and I teamed up against Charlie and George. I threw him countless passes that he routinely snatched from the air with increasing expertise. After each catch, Auggie made a jolting cut, a move I'm told he learned from the Madden video game, and then immediately rushed hard for the end zone. The days we could not cajole his brothers to play with us, Auggie and I often took to the park alone. We loved to practice the difficult fly route, although my poor timing on deep passes usually failed him. He ran, and ran, and ran again the distance of our makeshift field. If my deep throw dropped anywhere near his racing stride, he laid his athletic body out to make the dramatic catch. A metaphor for his many passions, Auggie loved to dive.

For some of the family games in the park, our border collie mutt dog Igor enthusiastically joined the fray as the fastest Hubbard defensive player. Whenever Auggie tried to run with the ball, Igor sunk his teeth into one of Auggie's flapping pant legs and refused to let him go; he loved to trip up his youngest brother. Eventually, nearly every pair of Auggie's jeans sported tears around the ankles. The fact that our playful puppy primarily tackled Auggie rather than Charlie or George formed the family theory: Igor must have thought he was son number three in the pecking order, with Auggie his subservient junior. This playful show of dominance ironically continued until little Auggie approached six feet tall. Auggie did not mind, of course; each time his dog latched on, he laughed and laughed. With a wide and joyful smile, Auggie yelled, "Igor!" as he tumbled to the ground.

Of course, the law of growing up requires that children eventually outgrow the treasured rituals they share with their parents. At some point, Auggie stopped begging me to throw him the football. What I would give if I had known precisely which game of catch in Windmill Park would be the last; I would have properly commemorated that nostalgic day of shared passion, reckless exuberance, and love.

—

In the fall of Auggie's seventh-grade year, our family drove back from Omaha after attending one of George's high school swim meets. As we neared Sioux City on our trek back home, Auggie begged me to stop at the mall.

"No," I stated. "I really want to get home. It's getting late."

"Well, I really want to see the new NFL-sized football that just came out."

"That's ridiculous. There is no reason to stop. We are not buying another one of those tonight. Maybe for your birthday next month?"

"I'm not saying you have to buy it. I just want to see it."

His irritating and persistent requests eventually wore me down. When we arrived in Sioux City, I took the exit to the shopping mall and pulled into the drop-off zone next to Scheels' main entrance. Without a word, Auggie bolted out of his seat and ran into the store. For five minutes I idled the minivan in our illegal parking spot while the older boys understandably complained. Then I heard the side door of our minivan slide open; from my rearview mirror, I watched Auggie climb back into his seat directly behind me. As he strapped his seat belt into place, I noticed the content expression on his round, red face. His eyes caught mine in the mirror.

"Thanks," he said. "I just needed to see it."

A month later, this time for his late December birthday, Auggie went berserk when he opened his present from Mom and Dad: another NFL-sized football.

—

Auggie played on the football team his freshmen year of high school, more out of historical obligation than desire. He always said he would be a professional wide receiver, the next Brandon Marshall, but his football obsession had mostly faded by the time his high school career began. When the shoulder pads and helmets joined the game, Auggie understandably discovered that he did not particularly enjoy being hit or yelled at. Increasingly awkward and reclusive, he also struggled to fit in with the other kids on the team. During games, April and I agonizingly watched our uncomfortable fourteen-year-old boy stand by himself on the sidelines in his football gear, ten or more feet from the regimented line of other players. By his sophomore year, he stopped watching Broncos games with me altogether; depression saw to that.

But by his freshman year of college, Auggie rejoined me in our Denver Broncos fandom. Since his brothers had left the cause almost entirely by then, I appreciated having someone to watch the games with. Regardless of the compounding struggles of his late teens, Auggie usually shared three hours with me on those precious Sunday afternoons. A time or two we even drove to a sports bar in nearby Le Mars if the local station did not broadcast the Broncos game. Together, we ate pizza, enjoyed the victories, and suffered the defeats.

One Sunday during Auggie's freshman year of college, I had to miss our regular Broncos date; I was driving back from North Dakota by myself after seeing a play that April directed up there. At his mom's request, Auggie called my cell to update me on the game that I was forced to miss. For more than two hours of my lonely stretch across the outback of the South Dakota prairie, Auggie provided play-by-play commentary on what turned out to be a Broncos loss.

The Turkey-Leg Hand

I'm trying my best to surrender to the dazzling corporate spell of the happiest place on earth. For her parents' fiftieth anniversary, April organized a Christmas trip to Disney World, an extravagant act of love, especially on professors' salaries. Growing up, April's workaholic farmer father rarely took vacations, but Disney World was an exception. Like so many members of Generation X, April grew up watching the *Wonderful World of Disney* every Sunday evening. So it was an especially meaningful gift to her and her siblings when their dad loaded them up into their family car and drove for three full days to the swamps of Florida over their Christmas vacation. Decades later, with her father now in poor health, my wife nobly strives to replicate this adventure for her aging parents and our boys. I'm not really a Disney guy, but I try to get in the spirit.

Today is water-park day at Blizzard Beach, a splashy wet-zone made to appear like a melting ski-resort. After spending the morning hurling our bodies down imaginatively engineered slides with thousands of other holiday thrill-seekers, we all gather to enjoy a lunchtime feast. Grandma, Grandpa, April, her brother, her sister and brother-in-law, and the five cousins convene around picnic tables in a pristinely landscaped outdoor restaurant. The table brims with food and stories of wet adventures on seemingly perilous slides. I can barely resist the temptation to calculate again the cost of the trip and how long April and I will need to work to pay off our share of this expensive fantasy. But then, with an impish grin, Auggie takes center stage and succeeds in making Disney World the happiest place on earth, indeed.

For his special holiday lunch, Auggie selected an enormous glazed turkey leg. After partially devouring the gigantic appendage, inspiration strikes. Our shirtless nine-year-old cleverly wraps tan napkins around his wrist in such a way as to conceal the seam between his actual skin and the turkey's great leg. Suddenly Auggie's right hand is not a hand at all, but a large, knuckleless, fingerless stump of partially eaten brown and pink turkey flesh. He gestures grandly with his glazed turkey-leg-hand as the rest of us try not to spit out our food. But our laughter doesn't come close to Auggie's glee at his own sight gag.

As Auggie waves around his fabricated deformity, he attempts to ad-lib about why a previously healthy hand has been replaced by a giant turkey leg. But his own giggles prevent coherent speech. Mirth radiates from our self-confident, jubilant boy in waves that rival even the most thrilling water slides and rides at Disney World. No cost, no future debt will come close to matching the payoff of this priceless moment.

Fifteenth Christmas
A North Dakota Carol

DECEMBER 24, 2014

Untamed by plows, snowdrifts creep over the prairie road that leads to the dying rural village of Edmore, North Dakota. Our minivan scrapes against the drifts, producing plumes of powder in our wake, as we drive the last lonely mile into town, or what used to be a town. Normally, we would stop first at Grandma's house for Christmas cookies and weak coffee. Bad weather has slowed our long trek from Iowa, forcing us to head straight to the Christmas Eve service. As it is, we'll arrive at the church about ten minutes late. Not too bad considering the weather.

"I wonder if the pastor will go all Tea Party on us again this year," says my seventeen-year-old son, grinning from the far back seat.

Our family has attended Christmas Eve services at the same Free Lutheran Church in Edmore, North Dakota, since our teenage boys were babies. My wife and I were married in this fundamentalist offshoot of the Lutheran Covenant, and the same soft-spoken minister who performed our wedding ceremony still presides—the conductor of countless well-meaning, joy-challenged services since. Remembered ghosts of Christmas sermons past include laments on the diabolical conspiracy to take Christ out of Christmas and how fantastically faith-filled America *used to be* before same-sex marriage and secret Muslims took God from the government. I was under the impression that God, an all-powerful being, couldn't be taken out of anything against his will. But oh well.

I do sometimes fear that my broad-minded take on the gospel has done a disservice to my three beautiful boys; I am light on brimstone and culture-war lingo and heavy on loving the sinner without automatically presuming the sin. Perhaps my hermeneutical suspicion inspired my youngest son, who just turned fifteen, to recently decree to his mother and me that he "doesn't believe in God anymore." He therefore should not be required to sacrifice precious Sunday mornings from his *League of Legends* training regimen, adhering to his parents' illogical pursuit of hypocritical holiness.

Only thirty minutes prior, as our nine-hour drive from Iowa to Grandma's house neared its end, I found myself physically wrestling a 2DS game system from my rebel child's furious fingers. This regrettably aggressive act came with the promise that he "wouldn't get it back either" unless he was "respectful and considerate at family activities." I added, "Grandma would never understand if you did not go to church with us." Has any parent ever failed so epically? At least our two older sons, more generous in spirit regarding the rigid religiosity of their Scandinavian forebears, retain their senses of humor about the upcoming Christmas Eve service. "Why can't everyone just be Episcopalian," jokes my fifteen-year-old as we bump onto the nearly empty parking lot servicing the nearly empty church. Kidding my bride, I repeat the phrase I say Every Single Time we visit the house of worship that hosted our wedding all those years ago: "the scene of the crime." No one ever laughs, and this time is no exception.

Twenty-some years earlier, this graded gravel lot proudly claimed thirty cars or more on Christmas Eve. Tonight, our minivan makes four. Like a hospice patient, the terminally ill church and the town in which it sits linger near expiration—too far gone to expect recovery except by way of miraculous intervention.

On this holy night, silent save the whistling prairie wind, we park our minivan and collectively stride through the polar air toward the church's double doors. As we near the threshold, a sense memory recalls these same doors swinging open on a sweltering August afternoon twenty-two years earlier, the day of our wedding. My gorgeous, Nordic bride with high, tear-stained cheekbones triumphantly exiting these doors beside a goofy young man who sort of looks like me, pelted by rice. Or was it birdseed? It was so hot in the nonair-conditioned church that day that I sweated through my cummerbund.

A burst of subzero air swiftly brings me back to the present as my bride and I—two decades later—struggle to pry open those same church doors for our freezing family. Leaning against the perpetual prairie wind, we press on through the narrow opening, our family spurting into the church cloakroom like pressurized toothpaste. With practiced efficiency, we deposit our North Dakota winter armor into the entryway, forming piles of polar-fill, wool, and fleece. Presentable at last, we collectively turn the corner toward the church sanctuary.

Of course, no good free-Lutheran would ever use the term "sanctuary" lest they invite the damnation of papist affiliations into their fundamentalist Protestant kingdom. But it's my word for the space. A solitary usher monitors our tardy arrival. The thick farmer's fingers of one of his hands clutch a stack of church bulletins—in the other hand is a bundle of LED penlights.

"LED lights?" I ask.

"Yeah, we're using these instead of candles for 'Silent Night' this year," he sheepishly offers while successfully avoiding eye contact. "It's better for the rug."

Throughout this brief exchange, I struggle to suppress the knowledge that, nine years earlier, this same gentle Norwegian farmer broke my father-in-law's heart and perhaps his health when he foreclosed on half of the remaining Blomquist family farm because a desperation loan could not be repaid. My proud father-in-law never truly recovered from that blow; he passed away just nine months ago from heart disease exacerbated by fettered dreams. His casket rested only feet from where we currently stand; tonight marks our first Edmore Christmas Eve without Grandpa Charles, the patriarch, in attendance.

"And, ah, this way the kids will get a keepsake," the gentle Norwegian farmer adds. By kids, he must mean my three giant teenagers (six two, six one, and five ten, respectively) plus the single little girl I notice nestled between her mother's ankles in the back row of the church. As near as I can tell, no other "kids" abide anywhere else in the vicinity. We all take a penlight.

The optimistically designed worship space of the Free Lutheran Church consists of a spartan altar abutted by ten rows of pews with a wide aisle running up the center. Each side of the aisle sits ten people in a pinch—twenty across if needed. If full, as I've seen it a time or two over the decades at weddings or funerals, this country church could comfortably accommodate over two hundred souls. Tonight, only the back row on the right side holds any occupants at all (eight adults plus the little girl). My beloved, introverted mother-in-law makes nine. She sits alone in the second-to-last row. She beams with joy at the long-awaited sight of her strapping grandsons and her beautiful daughter; she gently gestures her arms, shepherding the family to her open pew. The entire Christmas Eve congregation fills one side of two rows in the far back of the otherwise fallow church. Eight rows away, the lonely pulpit sits empty, at least twenty yards from the nearest heartbeat.

Our late arrival turns out not to be an issue. The pastor serves two congregations—a reality of prairie ministry in the depopulating American outback of rural North Dakota. The blustery roads must have slowed his journey from the Hampden congregation twenty miles away. Scored by the chorus of canned piano hymns, we all sit in a polite silence and stare at the egg-white portable projection screen that completely obliterates our view of the altar. To me, the screen is a bad sign. Pastor discovered PowerPoint a few years back. A preacher visibly terrified of public speaking, he now routinely distracts his audience from looking at him with blurry projections of religious memes and awkwardly spaced sermon outlines timed out with the technical precision of an infinite number of monkeys simultaneously typing out the book of Deuteronomy.

About fifteen minutes into our silent wait, an elderly widower slowly rises from his pew, steps into the aisle, and sheepishly clears his throat. "Considering the poor weather, will you all join me in a prayer for Pastor," he meekly requests. Fifteen heads politely bow. "Dear Jesus, thank you for this holy night. Thank you for being born into this world. Please watch over Pastor as he travels through bad weather. Protect him. Bring him home safely. In Jesus' precious name, Amen." As if in divine response, the side door nearest the altar pops open, revealing Pastor's round, pink face, circled by a fur-lined, South Pole–caliber parka. His thick mittens clutch a naked laptop computer to his chest as if for protection from the storm and our prying eyes.

"Oh my, so sorry I am so late," he offers. "The roads were not too good."

With unintentionally comic bumbling, the late sixty-something servant of the Lord fumbles for ten minutes or more trying to set up his PowerPoint display while the rest of us look on encouragingly. His millennial daughter eventually comes to his aid, troubleshooting connections between the computer and the projector, but to no avail. Moments before the flustered preacher calls quits on this attempt to merge worship with technology, the screen unexpectedly lights up—perhaps an answer to someone's prayer, although certainly not mine. An off-center clip-art image of a blue-eyed Jesus reaches outward to the Christmas Eve congregation like a hippy Uncle Sam. At last, the service can begin.

True to form, Pastor does his best to hide behind the wide podium that sits on the stage-left side of the altar framed by the obligatory potted fern. The low-fidelity microphone that curls over the podium like a slender shield even helps hide his face a bit. The microphone would not be necessary if the congregation did not deliberately choose to sit as far away as possible or if Pastor could project his naturally quiet voice just a few feet farther. As someone schooled in the realities of stage fright, my heart goes out to this introverted preacher every single time I see him on the pulpit—dozens of occasions over the years. He clearly tries so hard, prepares so much, but remains afflicted by the deep shyness and colossal reserve so prevalent among members of his Scandinavian brethren. Despite his kind eyes and pure motives, Pastor's preaching never fully overcomes the sense that this man lives under a veil of profound shyness.

And like so many of us shaped by the increasingly polarizing media narratives of our time, Pastor's theology has grown even more rigid than his delivery style. When I first met him for pre-marriage counseling nearly a quarter-century ago—a requirement to be married in my wife's hometown church—I recall respecting his authentic, conservative theology; I don't remember his religious beliefs then so perfectly adhering to the alt-right talking points of today. In recent years, he clearly chose to glean his sermon illustrations from a single news source. As a result, his lengthy sermons usually include diatribes against big government, the certainty of God's vengeful judgment upon most of the people not currently sitting in the room, the corrupting dangers of higher education, and the inscrutable fact that nearly every part of American life used to be better than it is today. Tonight's meditation even includes the lamenting phrase, "And things never change for the better, do they?"

What a hopeless sermon for Christmas Eve.

I resist the temptation to tune out, to let my heart grow hard to this gentle man and his stringent message. But, as someone partial to the traditions of the liturgical calendar, my ears prick up a bit when the word "Advent" enters Pastor's plainspoken lexicon.

"Advent is not a word you hear that much in our church," he muses. "It's not a bad word, really. It simply means 'coming.'" He continues in full North Dakota brogue: "Did you have an Advent wreath on your table when you were little before Christmas time? We did. Us kids useta fight about who got to light the candle each night. Did you know this tradition actually started in the Lutheran church in Germany in the 1700s? Yeah. I know we gotta be careful about putting too much stock on traditions that aren't in Scripture, but I think Advent candles are pretty good. As a boy, I remember learning that each candle stood for something: hope, love, joy, and peace. Well, I don't really know where all *that* came from, but I do know that when ya finally light *all* of the candles at the same time, on Christmas Eve, well, that's a lot of light at the supper table. It filled the room."

For a moment, Pastor seems freed from his notes, from the crutch of PowerPoint—which he has forgotten about and is now three slides behind—from his chronic timidity. Looking out to the congregation, he continues, emboldened, "The light of the candles is supposed to represent the coming of Jesus, I suppose. Kind of a welcome to him. No, it's more than a welcome, isn't it? Jesus *is* the light. He lights up our hearts. He lights up the world. He lights up . . . eternity. That's quite a welcome, if ya ask me. Do you ever wonder what the light of eternity might look like? It talks about it in Scripture, doesn't it?"

With practiced speed gleaned from years of guiding Sunday school kids through sword drills, Pastor locates Luke 2:12–14: "'And this shall be a sign unto you. Ye shall find the babe wrapped in swaddling clothes, lying in a manger.' Maybe we are not welcoming the baby Jesus so much as he's welcoming us? And it's a bigger welcome party than anything we could ever pull off. Even our best Christmas Eve supper would fall short, even with lutefisk smothered in white gravy, lefse fresh off of the griddle, and krumkake for dessert." After savoring a glance at his audience, he continues, "Now this is the part about 'light' . . ." His normally volume-challenged voice surprisingly soars beyond the inadequate microphone, almost filling the nearly empty church: "'And suddenly there was with the angel a multitude of the heavenly host praising God, and saying, Glory to God in the highest, and on earth peace, good will toward men.'"

In surprised expectancy, I lean forward, wanting more.

"Well . . . what was seeing the 'multitude of the heavenly host' like, anyhow, do you suppose?" he wonders. "Do ya think we can even imagine it? It was there, and it was gone, but it *was* there. The shepherds got a good look at it . . . the light of eternity. That's what Advent really welcomes, ya know, eternity. What will it be like to live in that light? I try to imagine it." He pauses as if unsure if he should share the impromptu image that has just popped into his mind: "Well, I think it might be a little bit like *The Lawrence Welk Show*."

This weird reference surprises me.

"Do you remember watching that program? They hardly show it anymore, do they? It's on sometimes, but not too much. Ya really have to look for it now, don't ya? My family all used to tune in to it together every Saturday evening. My whole family watched his show in the winter months, especially if there weren't too much farmwork to do. Anyhow, I kinda think that the 'multitude of the heavenly host praising God' might be a little like a really good episode of *The Lawrence Welk Show*."

The only thing keeping my teenage children's eyes from rolling through the back of their heads is the fact that they probably don't know who Lawrence Welk was, a squeaky-clean big-band leader known for his accordion playing. *The Lawrence Welk Show* ran on network TV and in syndication from 1955 until 1981. PBS picked up the reruns after that. The son of German immigrants, Welk grew up on a North Dakota farm not too far away. With a limited cadre of celebrities to choose from, his portrait still proudly hangs in the state capitol building in Bismarck, not far from Peggy Lee, Louis L'Amour, and Roger Maris. North Dakota royalty.

Known for its wholesome, easy-listening music, Welk's band played a mixture of polkas and show tunes. A time or two, my grandma tried to make my sister and me watch reruns of his show on PBS when she was babysitting. Even then, the music and visuals seemed painfully square. One critic in the 1950s called Welk's music as "light and bubbly as champagne"—a little ironic considering his popularity among teetotalers. Embracing the champagne metaphor, Welk incorporated a bubble machine into his act. He would start a musical number with his signature phrase, "And-a-one, and-a-two," as bubbles framed the band and his smiling troupe of conservatively clad ballroom-style dancers glided across the studio's stage with precision. Welk once reportedly fired a female dancer for too high a hemline. When the bubbles finally popped and the music swelled to its finish, this native North Dakota showman enthusiastically praised his ensemble, exclaiming, "WUNNERFUL, WUNNERFUL!"

I can only imagine how my Generation Z children would mock every feature of *The Lawrence Welk Show* should it somehow find its way onto one of their screens.

And yet, on this sacred night, the fresh image of a "Lawrence Welk Advent" gently works upon me, a positive force, a bubbly hope. The Holy Spirit must be at work; no other reasonable explanation exists. Sanitized polka music from the 1950s is certainly not my ideal glimpse of the kingdom of heaven. But through Pastor's relived immigrant story, I can suddenly taste the purity, generosity, and innocence of this bygone entertainment.

Like scales dropping from my eyes, I forget the strained theology of the rest of the sermon. I see beyond the hijacking of our intercultural gospel as a mandate for the American Dream; past the fear of the stranger justified as divine patriotism. As if against my will, the culture war recedes under the shtick of three quick steps and a hop danced to two-four time.

As if looking through one of those holiday snow globes, a scene appears in my mind's eye: Scandinavian immigrants in the early 1950s, perhaps Pastor's ancestors, perhaps my wife's, wearily enter a farmhouse after a hard day's work of trying to keep livestock alive through a bitter North Dakota winter; a family unit huddled together in the one warm spot of the house, probably the kitchen, gazing longingly at the magic box; fuzzy black and white images propel through the atmosphere of subzero prairie winds that rattle the windows with eerie shrieks; collectively, three generations tap their feet, smiling, embracing the joy of polka, of music unadulterated, of grace seeking expression; grandparents who don't speak English too good gently bounce toddlers on their knees; a palpable sense of nostalgic hope pervades . . . hope for a world that never really fully existed on this post-Fall forbidding prairie, but one ceaselessly yearned for and somehow remembered. We seek, all of us, our own version of a polka-dance party pervaded by joy, enveloped in love, and absent of fear.

Surely, over two thousand years ago, those frightened, bone-tired, poorly fed shepherds—themselves outsiders in their harsh and inhospitable community—witnessed their own culturally resonant version of the Lawrence Welk polka-dance party on that night, that holy night, when paradise opened before them, revealing "a multitude of the heavenly host praising God, and saying, Glory to God in the highest, and peace to his people on earth!" That night, a baby God birthed into our broken kingdom, a world full of humanity groaning for redemption and finally finding it among hay, sheep, manure, and in the protective arms of a young Palestinian-Jewish couple just trying to get by. Truly WUNNERFUL, WUNNERFUL!

When the sermon finally concludes, the natural reticence of my fellow worshipers prevents me from knowing if anyone else shared my glimpse of the polka Kingdom; I suspect they did not. As with every Christmas Eve service at this little church, we conclude by singing "Silent Night," illuminating the darkened, nearly empty space with our raised penlights gently waving in a ritualized welcome.

After the hymn, we form a short receiving line, filing one by one past the pastor in the rear of the church. As is his practice, he offers each parishioner a piece of chocolate as we pass, sweet sustenance for our life-risking journey into the forbidding winter blast that awaits. Ahead of me in line, my youngest son, Auggie, the searching soul currently trying on atheism, hastily shreds his wrapper and gratefully pops a Hershey miniature into his mouth. "Thank you," he says.

As Pastor hands me my treat, I truly want to hug the guy, but I don't. Instead, I thank him for his sermon, for his service, and silently pray that the gates of heaven will indeed open again soon, bathing us *all* in a holy transcendent light that will erase our disparities and fragilities, revealing our common humanity as image bearers of Jesus Christ, and forever heal our collective brokenness.

Amen.

The Family Business

As college theatre professors with a young family, April and I exploited our children.

They loved it.

It started because, as young parents, we genuinely wanted to spend as much time with our kids as possible. The long evening hours of a theatre life impinged on family time, so we put our boys in our shows when we could. We soon realized that casting our own children saved a fortune on babysitters during those unavoidable patches where April and I directed plays simultaneously. For my three-hour-long 2007 production of *The Grapes of Wrath*, our kids became migrant Okies. I established our own miniature Hooverville in my office just off the theater—a tent constructed from blankets and sheets brought from home. Our kids crashed under the makeshift camp at bedtime until later in the evening, when I carried their sleeping bodies in my arms to the car one by one.

This creative life produced many vivid memories. Our eldest son, Charlie, took his roles so seriously. In April's ambitious and magnificent 2004 production of Euripides's *Hecuba*, he was murdered offstage. A chorus of Trojan women carried his little body onstage wrapped in a funeral shroud. To make his performance seem more honest, Charlie, on his own volition, practiced keeping his chest from moving when he breathed. He acted so convincingly that I nearly rushed onstage on opening night to make sure my son was still alive; he was in kindergarten at the time. Another disturbing yet wonderful moment occurred when little George passionately yelled, "He's dying, I tell ya," in *The Grapes of Wrath*. His character was trying to convince the remnants of the Joad family to feed his starving father. A few moments later, George, a second grader at the time, gently looked on as the actress playing Rose of Sharon pretended to breastfeed his dying, onstage pa. Yep, the theatre life!

Only a toddler when all this started, Auggie played his roles as well. I still vividly recall his angelic round face fervently singing in the chorus of children in April's massive 2011 production of *The Secret Garden*. Likewise, the image of Auggie's compact sixth-grader body dramatically clinging to a fireman's coat during a chaotic crowd scene in his mom's production of *The Best Christmas Pageant Ever* survives as a cheery memory.

When Auggie was twelve years old, I cast him as Teiresias's boy in a futurist-dystopian adaptation of Sophocles's *Antigone*. For this silent role, Auggie guided his blind soothsayer master across the stage linked by a long hemp rope tied around both their waists. This production coincided with one of Auggie's obsessive reading phases, so he spent nearly every spare moment of the long backstage hours with his nose in a book. When he exhausted his supply from the school library, he precociously borrowed acting and directing books from my office shelves and devoured them in the theater wings. "What should I read next to become a great actor and director," he would ask as he returned to me his "empties." Again, he was twelve.

About two years after *Antigone* closed, Auggie's moody middle-school brain craved more diversion. I noticed from an audition flyer that a nearby professional summer Shakespeare festival was producing my favorite play, *Macbeth*. The announcement requested two child actors: an early teen to play Banquo's son, Fleance, and a younger child for young MacDuff. In a naked attempt to temporarily wean our obsessive son from his current and all-consuming

League of Legends addiction, I asked Auggie if he wanted to audition. A couple of weeks later, we found ourselves in a rehearsal room in Vermillion, South Dakota, negotiating with the festival's artistic director.

"Since we are going to need to drive Auggie an hour each way for every rehearsal," I self-servingly offered, "any chance I could take a role as well? I'll be here anyway, and I *am* a theatre professor."

I was secretly hoping the artistic director would cast me as Banquo so I could play Auggie's dad onstage and off, but she had other plans. I ended up serving as a utility infielder for the tragedy, playing multiple smaller parts, including a murderer who tries but fails to kill young Fleance in a dramatic nighttime ambush. For that scene, Auggie got to pretend to slice my hamstring with a dagger in self-defense, sending me to the grass writhing in pain. He maimed his would-be attacker with all the gusto you would expect from a boy who never did anything halfway.

The Worldwide Anglican Communion

A s a young boy, Auggie fully embraced the rituals of the Christianity in which he was raised. One Christmas season when he was seven years old, our family visited another church in town for reasons lost to time. Part of the evening service program included a Christmas pageant. At one point, a tired-looking assistant pastor addressed the congregation, beseeching, "Will the angels now take their places in the manger." Dozens of children with cardboard wings and tinsel halos embarked on the journey from their parents' hips to the front of the church. Before we could advise him otherwise, Auggie was in the aisle, totally unrehearsed for the task to come but eager and willing to contribute. He found a spot in the clump of kids and, with characteristic verve, belted out the chorus of "Silent Night" on-pitch and with authority. From his claimed position within the heavenly chorus, Auggie's round and serious face appeared more cherub-like than the other children actually dressed in angels' costumes that evening.

When Auggie believed in something, he committed; he threw himself into the breach.

Years later, when Auggie was in fifth grade, we once again found ourselves visiting a new church. The transition was painful yet welcome. The spiritual abuse my wife endured as an employee at the nearby Christian college eventually forced her to leave her job and, subsequently, the church our family had attended for a decade. But the opportunity to join the Episcopalians, the denomination that brought me into the fold as a teenager, partially redeemed our family's painful denominational transition. Church of the Savior was new and small—about twenty regular attendees—but refreshingly alive with zeal, and wit, and questions, and grace. After a few years of building hopping, the budding congregation landed in a converted two-bedroom residential home the Episcopal dioceses had purchased for them. So, one Iowa Sunday in January, we Hubbards found ourselves taking up an entire row in what was formerly a modest living room.

Episcopalians embrace their traditions more than most denominations. One tradition at Church of the Savior was to ask the youngest able member of the congregation to light the candles prior to Sunday worship and to put them out at the end of the service. On our first Sunday, our family watched a rambunctious preschool fellow named Truman eagerly tackle this important duty, with his father's assistance. On our second Sunday seven days later, the Truman show was not present. At eleven years old, Auggie accurately deduced that he was now the youngest present congregant; and without hesitation, he strode to the rear of the church where a philosophy professor and church founder handed him a brass candle-lighter and lit the wick for him. With no further instruction, Auggie strode to the altar armed with his flaming sword.

Our previous evangelical church did not embrace the many prescribed physical movements of high-church worship; they would likely consider them "too Catholic." So Auggie never experienced such formalities as weekly communion, kneeling for prayer, or genuflecting in the presence of the cross. But he must have carefully observed little Truman the previous week. When Auggie reached the altar with his lit wick burning, he first stopped dead-center and reverently bowed from the waist before the symbol of Christ's death and resurrection. He then carefully lit each of the candles on either side of the cross, returned to the center, and deeply bowed again.

—

In the years to come, even during times when Auggie's erratic moods drove him into isolation, even when he questioned or renounced his faith, our bold boy still occasionally volunteered to light the candles at the start of a service and snuff them out at the end. During his teen years, his mom and I never dared comment on or compliment our son's sporadic candle-lighting contributions, lest he become self-conscious and permanently end his service. But we silently watched his committed, full-body bows when confronting the cross, our hearts full and proud of our intense boy and his steadfast, public performance of supplication.

—

After we had attended Church of the Savior for only a couple of months, our priest asked the congregation if anyone present wanted to "be confirmed," to officially join the denomination, when the bishop came through for his annual visit. Nearly every member of this rebel church used to belong to another denomination. Before we left our previous church, our two older boys were on track for what the locals refer to as "profession of faith," the commitment ceremony most teenagers undergo in this heavily Reformed pocket of pious humanity. To our delight, our seventh grader and eighth grader both agreed to officially be confirmed in their new church. Still only in fifth grade, Auggie seemed too young for this midadolescence ritual. April and I decided that waiting a year or two would be better for him. For years, I regretted this decision.

On a rainy and muddy early spring day, the bishop of Iowa laid his hands on the brows of our two older boys, following the tradition of Jesus laying his hands upon the apostles. Auggie sat in the pew with visiting grandparents and watched. At the reception later that afternoon, I vividly remember Auggie picking at his potluck plate and wistfully mumbling, "I'm getting left out of everything." I hope I assured him that this wasn't true. At any rate, the years to come wreaked havoc on our plan for Auggie's spiritual development. First came teenage rebellion made more severe by what we now understand to be a diagnosis of high-functioning autism. Next, Auggie endured a five-year battle with major depression that zapped his hope and trust in eternity. Understandably, our boy therefore deferred subsequent, annual requests to confirm his parents' faith in our church. Although we still made him attend each Sunday, we dared not push for more.

That required attendance at Church of the Savior eventually regressed from passive compliance to active hostility. Auggie had become prone to mood swings. If a bad mood happened to hit on a Sunday morning, look out. In what I viewed at the time as an irritating performance but now see differently, Auggie would sit between his mom and me and brood. He slumped his body with his head down, and his long blond bangs that he refused to let us cut covered his eyes like Cousin Itt from *The Addams Family*. In such a small church, this rebellious presence was hard to miss, but nobody ever complained or even mentioned it. Despite his clear effort to make everyone know that he did not want to be there, Auggie remained welcome in this wacky, weird little church family. The warm response from our fellow brothers and sisters in Christ toward our struggling son softened April's and my apprehensions about forcing him to attend. He may not have cared, but at least they wanted him here.

His general disdain for church continued in various incarnations throughout high school. For Auggie, always a pursuer of truth, flirtations with cooler ideologies periodically replaced Christianity. Surrogate faiths in atheism or nihilism or anarchy or, most prominently, communism supplanted his complacent family's adherence to the silly myth of Jesus. Many of Auggie's unique cadre of social media influencers, we later learned, despised the church, or at least its more prosperity-driven, noninclusive cultural warriors. Even though our LGBTQ+ affirming congregation fit few of these negative stereotypes, Auggie still raged against the machine of corporate Christianity, political conservatism, and antigay evangelicalism.

Ironically, the introduction of a feisty rat terrier mix into our family may have prompted a slight softening of Auggie's negative attitude toward mandatory church attendance. As a gift for returning home from his third hospitalization for suicidal ideation, April and I agreed to get our seventeen-year-old son his very own "therapy dog." Of the many friendly and charming pups at the Sioux City Humane Society, Auggie picked out an ornery, creepy, black-and-white creature named Medea, appropriately named—by the Humane Society, we presume—after a murderous heroine in Greek mythology. The veterinarian estimated this tiny ball of fear and anger to be about four years old. Recently shipped from a pound in New Orleans, Medea was not housebroken, which led us to conclude that she had been homeless for all her life. In addition to needing expensive treatment for heartworm, Medea exhibited several odd and antisocial behaviors. The most irritating of these was her penchant for ferociously barking at anyone who came near her when she was sitting on Auggie's lap. She fervently protected him. But to her great credit, Medea loved to cuddle, to desperately press her bony little body against Auggie's chest. This trait helped us forgive her multitude of sins.

In commemoration of the Feast of Saint Francis, the patron saint of animals, most Episcopal churches offer a pet blessing on the first Sunday in October. In our little congregation, this annual event humorously became known as Bad Dog Sunday. As Bad Dog Sunday grew near, I reluctantly asked Auggie if he wanted to bring Medea to the service. Of course he did. Medea performed as expected that noisy Sunday morning. Pasted against Auggie's chest for over an hour, she snarled at the other dogs or cats or humans who dared make eye contact. But the sweet image of Auggie unself-consciously clinging to his dog throughout the service touched our hearts. We asked the priest if the little dog could attend other Sundays. She generously consented. For several weeks to come, Medea and Auggie clung to each other from the opening hymn through the closing announcements.

Near the end of high school, Auggie's negative attitude toward church tempered even more, a softening revealed through another odd tradition within our little church: the weekly practice of sermon discussions. Each Sunday, immediately after reading her sermon filled with thoughtful and erudite reflections on the prescribed Scripture readings, our priest stepped out from behind the lectern and invited "thoughts, comments, disagreements." For six years straight, Auggie remained silent during these wide-ranging and often challenging discussions of Scripture and theology. But, late in his senior year of high school, he started to ask questions.

"But how do we know God even exists?"

"Why would God think that throwing Jezebel out of the window to be eaten by dogs was somehow the right thing to do?"

"It seems to me like there are two Gods: the Old Testament God and the New Testament God. Why do we even care about Old Testament God? He seems pretty terrible."

"Shouldn't we forgive Judas?"

Satisfying answers to many of these provocative questions can be hard to locate. But to their credit, the priest and vocal members of the congregation responded to each of Auggie's probing queries with gentleness, consideration, and care; nobody present ever failed to listen or to take our son's theological wheel-turning seriously. And Auggie kept asking into his college years.

—

Like his brothers, Auggie attended college at the school where I teach. During his freshman year, he vacillated between academic successes and anxiety-induced failures, between intense excitement for his future and debilitating disappointment with his present, between a reckless joy for learning each morning and a consistent return of suicidal despair nearly every evening. On the advice of his psychologist, he started in the dorms, but he moved back home just three weeks into his first semester; the awkwardness of living in a small room with a fellow young man he did not know was too much for him. An impulsive, suicidal act caused him to nearly drop out in fall semester, but he somehow rallied and made the dean's list. But this struggle reversed itself in the spring as Auggie tumbled downward and ended up with a full medical withdrawal by midterm break.

Despite this academic roller coaster, college-Auggie almost always made it to church, even though we no longer required him to go. One day in September during his freshman year, the priest again asked if anyone in the congregation wanted to be confirmed when the bishop came through in November. College-Auggie, present and engaged, immediately raised his hand. The extremely permissive confirmation process in our little church involved the bare minimum of theological hoop jumping. People who wanted to join were asked to stay after church a couple of Sundays for discussions on church history and Anglican theology. To encourage my boy, I joined Auggie in these meetings, along with one or two other future Episcopalians. Always inquisitive, he politely engaged in the discussion. It seemed to matter to him.

That first Sunday in November, the bishop of Iowa again materialized in our tiny church. He wore his full regalia, so out of place in our converted living-room sanctuary: a bright red robe and a pointy mitre. With all the ceremony and liturgy of a cathedral service, the bishop laid his soft hands on Auggie's expansive forehead. With his shoulders slumped, as they often were in moments of mild social anxiety, Auggie dutifully repeated the poetic words from the Book of Common Prayer, an ancient ceremony of affirmation and belonging.

—

My theology may be hackneyed, or easy, or biased, or foolishly pacifying. Nonetheless, I believe that God unconditionally loved and *accepted* our tall, blond, handsome son for every moment of his nineteen years on earth. God loved and accepted Auggie *when* he leapt into the aisle at a strange church to vibrantly play his role in the heavenly chorus, when he reverently bowed at the waist when first lighting the candles at Church of the Savior, when he slouched in our row in church and hid his defiant eyes behind blond bangs of rebellion, when he fervently sampled the twentieth century's dominating anticapitalist political ideologies, when he intensely cuddled his feisty rat terrier on Bad Dog Sunday, when he asked his congregation how they knew that God even existed, when he bowed again in church, this time to accept the hands of the bishop of Iowa upon his forehead. I choose to believe that from Auggie's beginning until his earthly end, Jesus surely loved, welcomed, and accepted our beautiful boy as a full and privileged member of his body. A zealot with a checkered past, Saint Paul proclaims as much in his Epistle to the Romans: "For I am convinced that neither death nor life, neither angels nor demons, neither the present nor the future, nor any powers, neither height nor depth, nor anything else in all creation, will be able to separate us from the love of God that is in Christ Jesus our Lord" (Rom. 8:38–39 NIV).

—

So, it may have been a mere formality. Nonetheless, on November 3, 2019, on his own terms and with quiet integrity, Auggie officially joined the worldwide Anglican communion.

ACT II

The Family Monster

From Rage to Despair
(George's Warning)

As a child, Auggie's passionate nature heavily favored joy. But as adolescent hormones began to course through his body, the balance shifted toward rage. He had always been volatile, but by seventh grade his fits of anger carried the threat of menace. He more frequently and aggressively exploded, shouting, screaming, throwing things. Our hearts broke for him when, after failing to earn a desired score, Auggie impulsively smashed up his brand-new 2DS handheld video-game system, an expensive birthday present just a few days old.

Another day, he angrily stormed into his room after a fight with me and slung a book against his wall with all his might, shattering the glass of a framed picture of Jesus sitting in the garden with the little children that had hung in Auggie's sight for all his life. These new outbursts, we eventually realized, often came in response to a change in his expected schedule, especially my attempts to limit his *League of Legends* consumption. By year twelve, Auggie's bouts with rage devolved into colorfully cursing his perceived oppressors. In one vivid explosion, he shrieked at me, "I hope you die, you fucker!"

After family counseling failed, a diagnosis of autism, albeit high functioning, explained some of Auggie's increasingly frequent and uncontrollable bouts of rage. Between seventh and eighth grade, he blew up two to three times a week, mostly at me and my futile attempts to parent him. I tried and failed not to take it personally; I obviously did not know how to meet my son's unique needs. Auggie's antisocial tendencies also increased over this time. We begged him to attend his brothers' swim meets or soccer games. He loved music, but his increased social anxiety prevented him from crossing the street to watch a professional jazz band play in Windmill Park one summer evening. "I'll just watch them on YouTube," he offered when I tried to cajole him into the sunlight. Limiting his time with screens—their siren song promising a solitude both social and highly personalized—proved a constant battle.

While painful, maddening, and embarrassing, Auggie's increasing fits of fury soon became overshadowed by a more sinister threat to our family. A few weeks after Auggie started high school, his older brother George slid into a deep clinical depression. To our surprise and horror, suicidal thoughts plagued our high school junior, our gentlest boy. Auggie's profane bouts of rage, while unpleasant and disturbing, seemed trivial—even comical—in comparison to George's life-threatening suicidal ideation. April and I fell into reaction mode, triaging our children's most pressing needs, as the Hubbard family reeled between chaos and fear.

While distraught and frightened by George's descent, perhaps we should not have been surprised; mental illness knows our family well. My father, his father, his mother, and uncles and aunts on both sides of my family suffered from alcoholism; some died of it. My dad's disease forced him into homelessness near the end of his difficult and too-short life. Many of April's family proved predisposed to clinical depression and other related and undiagnosed strains of mental illness that manifested through obsessive behaviors such as paranoia and mania.

Like George, suicidal thoughts first visited April as a teenager. Over the decades, the family monster periodically raged then subsided in her life. Talk therapy and medications helped. The lowest point occurred in her early forties when a gatekeeping administrator at the Christian college where she used to teach bluntly told her that her permissive faith didn't belong in their tight Dutch cloister and openly plotted her removal. She fell apart. When she started fantasizing about turning the wheel of our Chevy Geo into oncoming semitrucks during her commute to work, April resigned her position and bravely checked herself into the behavior health hospital in Sioux Falls. In the years to come, our family would come to know that facility all too well.

A vivid memory from the early days of George's descent still haunts me. Before depression wrapped itself around his ankles, George loved to swim. During his sophomore year, he developed into one of the better high school swimmers in Iowa. We all looked forward to what he might accomplish in the pool his junior year, but depression stole that year from George. In addition to missing most of the academic season, he also stopped swimming.

One evening in February, after George had just returned home from his third hospitalization, I asked if he would go with me to lap swim at a nearby pool. An attempt to revive his love for the water. In the locker room after our swim, we chatted in vague terms about depression and his ongoing attempts at recovery. While stuffing his damp towel into his swimmer's gear-bag, George glanced sideways to me and prophesied, "We are really going to be in trouble when this hits Auggie."

A few months later, at the same age it hit George, depression settled into our youngest child's body and refused to go away.

Our Son the Communist
(Really)

During Christmas vacations, our family often spends part of the holiday with extended family in the Twin Cities. While there, we enjoy doing city things, especially seeing art-house movies. In 2015, a day after Auggie turned fifteen years old, we found ourselves at the historic Edina Cinema. Cousins, uncles, aunts, and grandparents converged on this little art-house multiplex in an inner-ring Minneapolis suburb to see a film entitled *Trumbo*.

Played by Bryan Cranston, Dalton Trumbo was a member of a group of blacklisted screenwriters and directors known as the Hollywood Ten. In 1950, Trumbo spent a year in prison after he refused to testify before Congress and was subsequently found guilty of contempt. We could have seen other movies this winter evening, but I suggested *Trumbo* because I guessed that Auggie might like it. Louis CK, one of Auggie's favorite comedians before he was canceled, had a small role. Little did I know.

Early on, Auggie's terrible mood promises to make the evening memorable for all the wrong reasons. Irritable, negative, and antisocial, our boy makes daily interactions with him harder and harder. In a futile attempt to serve as a buffer between him and less-experienced extended family members, I deliberately sit next to Auggie in those compact, old-fashioned movie theater seats. But my proximity irritates him. Before the previews even begin, Auggie barks at me multiple times to stop moving; apparently, I'm fidgeting in my seat. At one point, he even grunts, "Don't breathe on me." Irritated and lacking the necessary patience, I move a seat away, leaving an empty space between us in the darkening theater. It is that kind of night. Part of his surliness is surely normal teenage agitation with anything their parents do; part of it could be the autism only recently diagnosed; some of it, we now know, is the creeping effect of undiagnosed clinical depression afflicting our son's still-developing brain.

But beyond his unusually dark mood, this evening affects Auggie's life for years to come for reasons I never could have imagined. *Trumbo* sparks a quest for meaning deep within our boy. I imagine this conversation in the movie between Trumbo and his young daughter was the catalyst:

DAUGHTER: Are you a communist?

TRUMBO: I am.

DAUGHTER: Is that against the law?

TRUMBO: It is not.

DAUGHTER: The lady with the big hat said that you are a dangerous radical. Are you?

TRUMBO: Radical. Maybe. Dangerous. No. It's a good country. But anything good could be better, don't you think?

DAUGHTER: Is Mom a communist?

TRUMBO: No.

DAUGHTER: Am I?

TRUMBO: Well, why don't we give you the official test. Mom makes your favorite lunch . . .

DAUGHTER: Ham and cheese.

TRUMBO: Ham and cheese. And at school, you see someone with no lunch at all. What do you do?

DAUGHTER: Share.

TRUMBO: Share? Well, you don't just tell them to go get a
            job?
DAUGHTER: No.
TRUMBO: Oh . . . you offer them a loan at 6 percent? Oh,
            that's very clever.
DAUGHTER: Dad . . .
TRUMBO: Ah, then you just ignore them.
DAUGHTER: No.
TRUMBO: Well, well. You little commie.[4]

It takes a few months for April and me to realize the imprint
this tender scene left upon our sensitive and intellectual teenager.
We later learned that it spurred Wikipedia searches for summaries
of *The Communist Manifesto* and *Das Kapital*; a heartfelt awaken-
ing that the powers that be do an inadequate job of taking care
of poor people; and, eventually, indoctrination through voluntary
immersion into marginally insidious Reddit pages and niche You-
Tube channels. Before April and I realize what is even happening,
our fifteen-year-old son, in his desperate search for salvation for
himself and for the global poor, proudly and defiantly proclaims
to the world that he is a communist.

Having a self-proclaimed teenage communist living in the most
conservative enclave of Iowa is pretty damn funny, almost charming, until it isn't. For communism to take root in Auggie's justice-
seeking mind, history required rewrites. To secure future utopia, the
twentieth-century narrative cannot contain imperfections and certainly held no room for atrocities. To my horror, Auggie soon aligns
himself with fringe Internet activists who deny Stalin's murderous
acts. He parrots blinkered arguments defending China's response
to the Tiananmen Square protest and the "reeducation" camps that
followed. A chill overcomes me during dinner one evening when
discussing a deplorable school shooting in Miami. Over his plate
of spaghetti, our formally peaceful child, a boy who had never even
held a firearm much less shot one, informs the family that he does

not support gun-control legislation because the population will need automatic weapons to overthrow the government when the revolution comes. When one of his brothers challenges this call to violence, Auggie flies into a shouting rage.

To be fair, stubbornness is a family trait. Although far from an ambassador for laissez-faire capitalism, I find it impossible to sit quietly when Auggie denies the existence of Stalin's gulags or defends the Soviet military response to the Prague Spring. And, for long stretches, communism is all Auggie will talk about. We argue too much, and April has to remind me to play the adult. One night, during another visit to the Twin Cities, I have to leave a restaurant and stand on the street by myself while the rest of the family finishes their pizza because my youngest son will not stop needling me.

Eventually, I devise a rule. I will discuss Auggie's procommunist views and watch more of his YouTube videos *after* he reads curated selections from dissident writers. At first, he consents, and I give him my copies of Alexander Solzhenitsyn's *One Day in the Life of Ivan Denisovich* and Václav Havel's "The Power of the Powerless." But Auggie backs out of our agreement after fanatical members of a procommunism subreddit fervently warn him against reading work by turncoats like Solzhenitsyn and Havel lest he be crushed by the cogs of the sellout, anticommunist, imperialist propaganda machine.

At first, we suspect—and hope—this communism fixation will only be a phase, like previous obsessions with the Accelerated Reader program at school, football, *Star Wars*, Nerf guns, and *League of Legends*. To our dismay, however, Auggie's commitment to communism intensifies over the years. From that first evening after his fifteenth birthday when *Trumbo* lit the match, through high school and into his sophomore year in college, our son zealously confesses his unique understanding of the doctrines of communism to anyone who will listen—and also those who won't. Such commitment requires impressive integrity in our conservative little town. Among other colorful eccentricities, our irascible boy becomes known for the hammer and sickle screensaver proudly displayed on his high school–issued laptop.

As his fervor grows, so does his rigidity. Auggie strategically avoids even artistic representations of communism. I try to get him to read George Orwell's *Animal Farm* with me, but he refuses; he does not appreciate what he takes as manipulative allegorical satire. April barely prevents him from walking out of our family viewing of the Coen brothers' film *Hail, Caesar!*; he resents its playful depiction of 1930s communists. On another visit to the Twin Cities, Auggie flat-out refuses to see the critically acclaimed anachronistic comedy *The Death of Stalin*. While his brothers and I enjoy the film, he defiantly watches another movie at the cineplex with his more understanding parent. Entering college, he falls in love with Chaim Potok's beautiful novel *The Chosen*, a required summer reading in his first-year seminar. I immediately lend him a copy of my favorite Potok book, *My Name Is Asher Lev*, but Auggie abruptly stops reading after a Jewish character who survived a pogrom makes a negative statement about Stalin. That same year in college, Auggie considers majoring in political science, but he refuses to take any classes in this subject area for fear that his brainwashed, PhD-holding professors might fail to appreciate the elegant perfection of the influential theories of Marx and Engels.

Throughout this entire obsession, I struggle and fail to show respect for my son's opinions. Luckily, years of therapy combine with growing maturity to make Auggie's explosive blowups much less common, thank God. But I truly fear that some of his beliefs may be downright dangerous. Unfortunately, we both slip up on an August evening before Auggie's sophomore year in college. This time, our conversation devolves into a yelling match over China's treatment of the Uyghurs. I am most to blame for breaking the rule that prohibits talking about such things with him and for escalating tensions by raising my voice. In a fight-or-flight response,

I struggle to not shout when being shouted at. After cooling down by taking a walk around the block, I meekly return home and descend the stairs to the basement to apologize.

I find Auggie staring at a blank computer screen, perhaps considering whether to comfort himself with a video game. With humility fueled by shame, I put my hand on my son's slumped shoulder and say, "I am so sorry I yelled. I should not have done that. We broke our rule. We just can't talk about certain things. Please know that I love you, my sweet boy. Even though I disagree with you on some things, I love you. I do. I believe that your motives are good—both of our motives are good—but it's clear that we just can't talk about certain things without escalating."

Clearly distressed by our argument and my apology, Auggie turns his head toward me, his large blue eyes glossy with impending tears. "I'm sorry I yelled at you, Dad," he says. "I didn't mean to. I'm so afraid of what will happen to me if I stop believing that communism can save the world. What if none of it will work? What if the world can't be saved? Be better than it is? What if people will always suffer no matter what we do?"

"You are not alone in that fear, my boy."

"I get so mad because I can't handle how unfair, how unjust the world is, how much suffering there is. And I know, I know that a system exists that could help if we could only all agree to follow it. Why do we have to be so selfish? Why do rich people need so much stuff when most of the world suffers with nothing? I only want poor people to have what they need, that's all."

He turns his face back to the blank computer screen and continues, "Like we talked about in church a few weeks ago. Remember that reading from the book of Acts? It is so clear. We are all supposed to work together and share what we have, right? 'All things in common,' right? 'Sharing with anyone who might have need,' right? Why can't we do that? I need to believe that we can do that. I want to be happy; I want everyone to have what they need and to be happy."

I hug my son, pressing my cheek against the side of his face as he sits in the chair still facing the blank screen. He lets me hold him. I feel his tears dampen my face. Eventually, I lift my head, stare at his profile, and squeeze my hands on both of his shoulders. With a cracking voice, I profess, "I'm so proud of you, Auggie, of who you are. I should be more like you."

The All-State Redemption

The cast of Arthur Miller's *The Crucible* shift their weight in a groggy circle at nine fifteen on a surprisingly bright Saturday morning in October. In dutiful preparation for the three-hour rehearsal to come, I had just finished leading the actors through some warm-ups and theatre games. Now is prayer time, a cherished tradition at the small Christian college where I have taught theatre for the past seventeen years. The popcorn prayer includes petitions for sick roommates, unemployed parents, and enough energy to make it through upcoming midterm exams. After a pause, I sheepishly offer my own supplication. I normally refrain from sharing personal prayers during this student-centered ritual, but not today. Surprised by the emotion in my voice, I crackle, "Please, Lord, help my sweet son Auggie do well at his All-State auditions this morning."

This unusually warm autumn day marks the culmination of three years of obsessive anticipation followed by impending disappointment. As the cast of college actors prepare to run through Arthur Miller's foreboding classic, Auggie, now a senior in high school, figuratively endures his own crucible in a high school gym eighty miles away. Sitting next to his mother, who drove him there because he was not permitted to travel with the other students, our boy anxiously awaits his last chance to audition for Iowa's most celebrated high school music competition. *Dear Lord, help him.*

—

Our tuba player first auditioned for All-State three years earlier at the start of his sophomore year. Auggie had already earned first-chair tuba in the high school band his freshman year, an impressive underclassman achievement in our marching band–obsessed little town. In Orange City, almost every public-school kid joins the band. Families with high school students voluntarily forsake August vacations so their children do not miss mandatory band camp. Due to a lack of air-conditioning, the high school often cuts its classes short in the hotter days of early fall. Only the band receives an exemption since no principal would dare inform the iconoclastic band director otherwise. And, on Friday nights, the crowd at home football games hilariously decreases by 75 percent immediately *after* the intricate marching band halftime show finishes. It's that kind of town.

So, despite his youth, Auggie's singular desire to take the next step in his musical development by auditioning for All-State made sense. The audition required learning all the scales and mastering a preselected étude. A more connected band-parent informed me that the tuba section in our district only permitted three spots in a typical year, and over twenty tuba players showed up at the regional audition. So, when we learned that Auggie made first alternate on his first attempt, we beamed with pride for our fifteen-year-old tubist: "What a great start, Auggie! You'll get in for sure next year!"

—

When reflecting on the past decade, April and I regrettably use the anagrams "BD" and "AD" to divide the time: "Before Depression" and "After Depression." The insidious disease latched on to both of our younger boys as they approached sixteen. By the time All-State auditions rolled around that fall semester of his junior year, Auggie had already been hospitalized once for suicidal ideation and was attending weekly therapy sessions in Sioux Falls. Understandably, not much tuba practicing occurred during this terrible time. Like nearly every meaningful activity in his life, tuba playing receded in importance compared with the daily struggle to stay alive. In the fourth week of September, depression pulled our boy under yet again, forcing us to repeat the terrible eighty-mile drive to a behavioral health hospital in Sioux Falls, a duffle bag packed with clothing and toiletries hidden in the trunk.

During visiting hours on one of our daily trips to the Sioux Falls hospital, Auggie surprised me with a question: "Can I play my tuba here?" At an institution with intentionally thin walls where residents may not even wear shoes, I assumed the answer would be no, but I asked anyway. After some consideration, a sympathetic manager consented. Auggie could play his tuba while in in-patient care under the following conditions. First, we must bring the tuba with us and without its case each time we visited; it could not stay at the hospital. Second, April or I must always stay in the room with Auggie while he practiced.

Although April made the drive to Sioux Falls by far the most, the very next visit fell to me. Even without its case, the mammoth tuba barely fit into our subcompact hatchback Fiat. I could only wedge it in if I pushed the front seats all the way forward, which meant chewing on my knees for the 160-mile round-trip drive. Once I arrived, I conspicuously hauled the massive, naked instrument through multiple security checkpoints at the in-patient behavioral health-care center, which involved punching secret codes into unresponsive keypads at each new door.

"Yes, they told me I could bring this tuba to my son. You can check with them if you want."

"No, I can get it by myself, but it would help if someone held the door; we don't want any more dents."

This five-minute trek was made more difficult by my fumbling efforts to simultaneously carry a melting vanilla ice-cream shake from Five Guys that Auggie requested along with the tuba's massive mouthpiece, which needed to be carried separately because it would not stay in the tuba.

As soon as we were in the private room, Auggie took the mouthpiece from my sticky hand, buzzed it against his lips, and eased it into its designated slot. He then embraced the tangled web of dented and corroded brass that the high school had lent him and set himself about filling the air with its majestic and sonorous vibrations. He played an hour straight. I loved that he neither considered nor cared that every other troubled soul on that locked-down adolescent hospital ward must have heard and felt each booming, mournful note.

"Do you think I could be out of here in time to make All-State auditions?" Auggie asked during his second reunion with the tuba.

We checked, and the current plan of treatment called for Auggie to be released the day before All-State auditions were scheduled. Of course, April and I wanted him to audition, but we also feared that the added pressure might be too much in his current, fragile state. With apprehension, I swung by the high school band room the following day to pick up the music book from the head band director that contained the étude audition piece.

The next week of daily visits with Auggie up in Sioux Falls contained very little talking. In intensely meticulous ninety-minute rehearsal sessions, all his breath and energy during our visits went into mastering the difficult audition piece. As the week progressed, April and I enjoyed hearing the piece of classical music come to life via our son's brain, his fingers, and his heart. By the end of the week, it sounded so beautiful, full, and hopeful. Although we still feared that the pressure of auditioning could be unhealthy, April and I convinced ourselves that this vital form of music therapy compensated for the impending stress of competition. He needed something to look forward to.

Early on a gray and unfriendly Saturday morning in October, we dropped our high school junior off in the parking lot next to the band room. Having been released from the hospital just the previous afternoon, Auggie had not even returned to classes yet. Along with a select few other promising musicians, he loaded himself and his tuba into the van that would transport them all to the All-State auditions in nearby Storm Lake. Although we wanted to go with him, to support him, to protect our fragile boy, we were informed that parents did not attend All-State auditions.

We thought constantly about Auggie on that hopeful, stressful Saturday. We prayed throughout that morning that he would be okay, that the audition would go well, that he would make the band. We cautiously texted for updates. When April's phone buzzed with a call early in the afternoon, we both flinched in anticipation.

"How did it go?" April asked.

"Not so well," Auggie replied with surprising calm. "I didn't make it."

It turned out to be much worse than that. Through some terrible miscommunication, which I still struggle to let go of, Auggie learned the wrong audition piece. Because of his hospitalization, this unfortunate mistake was not detected until his head band director heard him warming up in the high school gym in Storm Lake minutes before his audition time.

I still wonder why in God's name the band director didn't immediately go to the judges and explain this unique situation. Why didn't he explain that this brave boy had left the mental hospital only the previous day? Explain that he accidently learned the wrong étude! Explain that this was not his fault! That it was an honest mistake! In the name of all that is good and holy, why wasn't someone looking out for Auggie and why did that person not ask, *no*, *beg*, the judges, the officials, the governor of Iowa, to please let this talented teenager play for them the beautiful piece of music he had so diligently prepared under such difficult circumstances? Even if they still saw fit to disqualify him, at least Auggie could have shown what he could do on the dented, tangled, hand-me-down web of brass and valves.

Instead, the band director handed our son the correct étude and told him that he had fifteen minutes to learn it. Auggie tried, I'm told. He must have fretted, but he tried. People who were there reported that he never panicked. The task, however, was too much, the music too difficult for even a gifted high school player to sight-read, to master without a single real rehearsal. In the end, Auggie played an étude that he did not know to judges who did not know his circumstances, and he did not make the band.

—

The start of a new school year often triggers suicidal thoughts in depressed children. The adolescent wing of the Sioux Falls behavioral health hospital always reaches capacity during the first week of September, we were told. During the start of his senior year, Auggie predictably struggled. He had already been hospitalized four times by that point, and he so wanted to avoid going back. Although more irritable and volatile than normal, he dedicated his limited energies that fall to staying out of the hospital. Auditioning for All-State proved a strong incentive.

We learned from Auggie's dedicated psychologist that planning for the future could sometimes mitigate depression's pull. The fall semester overwhelmed our struggling son with questions: Would he be able to make up all the coursework that he missed his junior year? Would he be able to go to college? Or would all the bad things keep happening again and again no matter what he did? Would there be a place for him in this world? Could he survive? For Auggie, practicing his tuba served as a temporary reprieve from these pressing anxieties; it was a distraction, a survival mechanism that kept uncertainty at bay—at least temporarily.

Over the summer, Auggie diligently practiced his tuba for an hour each morning and an hour each evening. We gladly drove him to Vermillion for lessons with a regional tuba expert when he requested more training. Every note of every scale filled the house with beautiful precision, over and over. And let me tell you, he played the correct fucking étude technically perfectly and with deep feeling. American culture conditions parents to make stupid and untrue proclamations to their children like, "You can do anything that you set your mind to" or "Hard work will always pay off." Such platitudes probably cause more damage than good in this rigged and disparate world. Nonetheless, I irrationally prayed, "Please, please, please, Lord, let this work pay off for Auggie. He's lost so much already. Let him have All-State."

A deeply unsatisfactory answer to this prayer seemed to arrive on a Wednesday morning in October two days before the scheduled All-State audition. I received a frantic phone call at work from the high school secretary informing me that there had been an incident after marching-band rehearsal and that Auggie had left campus without permission. Since I had walked to work, I immediately called April, who quickly jumped in the car to search the streets for our son. Two blocks from our house, she saw Auggie storming down the sidewalk. She drove beside him and slowed the car. Through the window, his face glowered red with unrepentant rage.

The incident, as we deciphered it, happened something like this. The rain that morning pushed the marching-band students off the football field and into the band room ahead of schedule. While the students reconvened inside, the head band director stayed on the field for a time to make sure the percussion equipment was safe from the rain. After putting his tuba away, an unsupervised Auggie discovered the attractive nuisance of the trap set used for the jazz band sitting unattended. He had been allowed to play the trap set in the past, but the band director had recently forbidden him to touch it.

Apparently, no matter how much he was warned, Auggie could not keep from banging on the drums with a force that might damage the set, to say nothing of the deafening noise. Unsupervised and surrounded by his peers, Auggie started playing those drums. A few seconds into his loud impromptu recital, the aggravated head band director appeared. He angrily stormed to the trap set and yelled in Auggie's face, "Get off of the drums!"

I can understand why he yelled; I too have yelled at Auggie in moments of frustration and weakness. I learned the hard way that this aggressive shouting never yields a positive result. A Molotov cocktail of surprise, embarrassment, depression, and aggravated autism ignited within Auggie's brain. In a rage, he stood up, pushed the smaller band director out of his space, shouted a threatening profanity, and stormed out. Dozens of bandmates witnessed it. And later that day, just two days before Auggie's final audition date for All-State, our senior son was suspended for a week, including from all extracurricular activities.

After getting the call from the assistant principal about the suspension, I slowly climbed the stairs to Auggie's room, where he had retreated to seclusion in his rage. My heart ached over the implications of the blowup. I opened his door and found Auggie covered head to toe by his comforter. My gentle movement of the top edge of the blanket revealed his face etched with agony. As if aware of the situation, his loyal rat terrier, Medea, at the time fervently buried into Auggie's chest and neck, growled at me in solidarity with her boy. The anguish on his face—regret and self-loathing—had completely erased the rebellion and self-righteousness he felt earlier.

"Why did I do that? I am so sorry," he offered, his eyes still pressed shut in torment.

"There will be time for apologies," I said. "Unfortunately, there will first be some difficult consequences." After I told him that the suspension included the upcoming All-State audition, Auggie's body seemed to collapse further into itself. He moaned. Moaned. I feared for his safety. With his jaw racked with tension, he repeated, "Why did I do that?" followed by "I worked so hard."

"Auggie, everyone in the world makes mistakes," I said. "And you are already forgiven. Please know that." Without thinking things through, I added, "I don't know if Mom and I have the power to help, but we are going to try to talk to the head principal and the band director to see if there is any way that they will reconsider letting you audition for All-State . . . if that is what you want." As soon as I offered this possible option, I regretted it, fearing the creation of false hope.

For the first time during this conversation, Auggie opened his eyes. Staring intensely at the light fixture on the ceiling, he asked, "Do you think they would?"

"I don't know. Probably not," I conceded. "But we will ask. We will try."

He then fixed his huge blue eyes upon me. With a voice not much above a whisper, he asked, "What will happen to me?"

I could tell from his tone that this question reached far beyond the current moment. My answer came quickly and surprised me.

"You just finished reading *The Sun Also Rises*, right? You like Hemingway. He has a famous definition you might appreciate about what it means to be brave. Hemingway defined true courage as 'grace under pressure.'"

"I didn't show much grace under pressure today. I lost it."

"I don't think that's what Hemingway meant," I answered. "Maybe he meant that a person should be judged by how they act *after* they screw up, not before. Listen, we all make mistakes. We all mess up. But how do we respond? Maybe that is more important. How do we show grace and humility and love when we don't feel like we deserve it? When we feel most ashamed? Listen, I am so sorry and so sad that this terrible thing happened today, Auggie. I'm sorry that you lost your temper. I know you didn't mean to. I'm not even sure you can help it. I'm just so sorry. But here is what I'm wondering now. I'm wondering if you can use this terrible experience to reveal the person who you truly are, the person who you want to be, the person who I know you are, by how you react to your mistake. You are under great pressure now, my boy. How can you show grace under all this pressure? It may be the best measure of a person."

April and I met the next day with the head principal and the assistant band director. To his credit and our gratitude, the head principal had previously gone to great lengths to academically accommodate both George and Auggie during their long battles with depression. The assistant band director met with us because the head band director, we were told, was still too shell-shocked from the incident the previous day. After some discussion, the principal graciously agreed to overrule the assistant principal's decision and let Auggie attend All-State auditions. The rationale was that All-State was a special case, separate from normal high school attendance and activities. The one provision was that Auggie could not go to the auditions in the high school van, nor could he eat with the other students or interact with them in any way during the festival. If one of his parents agreed to take him and supervise him, Auggie could audition.

—

As I tried to distract myself by watching the first off-book run-through of *The Crucible*, April accompanied Auggie to All-State auditions in Storm Lake. Upon arriving in the crowded high school gymnasium, Auggie and April found a safe place to rest his tuba. They then tried to decipher the complicated schedule posted on the cinder-block wall. As they scanned for Auggie's name, the assistant band director appeared behind them, voluntarily breaking the rule that there would be no contact between the black sheep tuba player and the rest of his high school contingent. The assistant band director helped Auggie locate his audition room and time on the massive schedule. He then awkwardly yet graciously tried to chat with April for a bit before wandering back to the opposite side of the gym where the rest of Auggie's high school classmates camped.

From across the crowded room, Auggie noticed the head band director whom he had shoved and cursed two days before. "I need to speak with Mr. ——," he gently told his mother. Before she could remind him that this was not allowed, Auggie boldly walked across the gym, his frightened mother in tow. When they arrived beside the head band director, he was in conversation with a colleague from another school, but April did report that she noticed his eyes flare open with fear when he realized who was standing beside him. He kept talking to his colleague for a minute or so while Auggie awkwardly yet patiently waited. Finally, the colleague stepped away, allowing Auggie to look directly into the eyes of the young teacher, the educator who ironically first suggested that Auggie pick up the tuba six years prior. The band director started to back away, but Auggie stopped him with his tender yet determined voice.

"Mr. ——," he petitioned. "I need to apologize to you. I am very sorry. I was completely wrong. I hope that you will be able to forgive me."

Blinking in awkward surprise, the band director sheepishly replied, "Thank you, Auggie." After a frozen moment of mutual unease, they stepped apart, each moving back to their respective camps.

Auggie then mechanically ran through his tuba warm-ups in a practice room. With plenty of time to spare, April helped him locate his assigned audition room from the many possible classrooms. They both took a seat along a row of chairs that helpfully lined the high school hallway. April sat closely beside her boy, consciously beaming him all her positive maternal energy. As they waited for his name to be called, Auggie confided, "I am really scared, Mom."

At this moment, another high school employee appeared: the matronly choir teacher. Her personality offers a working case study of what Saint Paul must have meant when he tried to explain the fruits of the spirit to the Galatians. Unlike some of the other teachers from Auggie's high school, she never tried tough love on him. In four years of choir, this dedicated and nurturing educator always showed compassion for our eccentric son, always rooted for him, and always refused to judge him. In the crowded hallway, this lovely, calming, public high school teacher stood over our son as he sat helplessly. She looked deep into his worried eyes and asked, "Auggie, may I pray for you?" A little embarrassed but willing, Auggie replied, "Yes."

The choir director then laid her hands on our boy's perpetually slumped shoulders and offered a simple yet elegant blessing. When she finished praying but before she removed her hands, she again peered deep into Auggie's huge blue eyes and said, "You are amazing." Soon thereafter, with his massive tuba in his arms, our battered boy stepped into his audition room alone. The door closed behind him.

—

On my walk home after my *Crucible* rehearsal, I step out of the crisp fall sunlight of the early afternoon and into the fluorescent lighting of our local pharmacy. Since April is out of town, the task of picking up Auggie's antidepressants before the pharmacy closes for the weekend falls to me. As I wait my turn in line, my phone buzzes. I pull it out of my front pocket to see April's picture flashing on the screen.

"Hello," I answer, my voice arrested with fear.

"Someone wants to tell you something," April's voice replies. A second passes.

"Dad?" Auggie asks.

"I'm here."

"I made All-State."

What a spectacle I make of myself; how strange I must appear to the fellow drug-seekers in the Dutch Mill Pharmacy. After hearing Auggie's good news, I find myself literally on my knees on the carpeted pharmacy floor. "Yes!" I shout at the top of my lungs for all the world to hear. "Yes!"

"Light"

Tom Kitt and Brian Yorkey's Pulitzer Prize–winning rock musical *Next to Normal*[5] tells the story of a suburban family ripped apart by chronic mental illness. And it's my theatre department's winter 2018 production. Because of a complicated scheduling issue, I only have four weeks from start to finish to direct this difficult show; and the crazy timetable includes musical and technical rehearsals. To fit everything in, we rehearse four hours a night, five nights a week, with another long rehearsal on Saturday mornings.

During this burst of artistic work, I usually grab Subway from across the street for supper that I wolf down at my office desk. On better evenings, April brings me a home-cooked meal lovingly transported in reusable plastic containers. While such a schedule is far from ideal, April and I both understand that our lives in the theatre occasionally require these sprints. It will be over soon.

After the long rehearsals, I drag my tired posterior home, a six-block walk from the theater building to our front door. The exterior of our house usually comes into view around 11:30 p.m.; streets lights illuminate pools of beige on the Craftsman exterior. Even though I spent my entire evening intensely wrestling with the fictional realities of clinical depression and bipolar disorder, I wince when my own house appears in the darkness. With a mixture of shame and relief, I acknowledge an ironic truth: my long evening trying to tame a heartbreaking tale about mental illness spared me from the gloomy, nonfictional truth of a night in a house of pain. My house.

By objective standards, things have sucked for three years straight since our middle son George first started showing signs of major depression. Then our youngest, Auggie. After medically withdrawing from his freshman year of college, George recently left a full-time, stand-in job working at a local factory. Seized again by his unrelenting depression, he simply could not make himself go to work anymore. During the weeks I work on *Next to Normal*, George barely leaves his room.

As difficult and upsetting as George's long struggles with depression are, the hellish force that threatens Auggie demands most of our attention. In the last two years the principal at his school has called us twice to report that the high school Internet filter flagged Auggie's Google requests seeking effective methods to commit suicide. He's been hospitalized three times for suicidal ideation. There will be more to come. On a family vacation in the Black Hills, I stand as close as possible to Auggie during our hike up Black Elk's Peak because he earlier threatened to throw himself off a ledge if we forced him to go.

Every week we spend half a day driving to Sioux Falls for cognitive behavior therapy that showed initial promise but no longer helps at all. There are multiple unsettling and risky chemical experiments with completely, fucking ineffective medications. Each change sends Auggie into a new petrifying spiral. His depression-fueled irritability combined with the rigidity of his autism makes the specter of a screaming fight at any moment an omnipresent menace. He calls from high school almost every day, pleading with us to let him come home early. Auggie stops practicing tuba altogether.

For the past few weeks, my demanding *Next to Normal* schedule temporarily excuses me from depression's daily duties. The guilt I feel about leaving April to go it alone balances against an embarrassing yet profound sense of relief. I am so tired. I will gladly work a fifteen-hour day just to earn a brief break from the house of pain.

But just as a single candle casts more light in a darkened room, brief relieving moments illuminated the otherwise consuming darkness of these years. Like grace-fueled bonfires, these merciful blazes conquered the night, if only temporarily.

FEBRUARY 2016

The first major wave of depression hit Auggie early in his sophomore year of high school. From there forward, he could not shake a dreadfully foul mood that infected most interactions; he talked often about the pointlessness of life. In a minor miracle, George, by then technically a senior in high school, rejoined the swim team after missing his junior season battling his own depression. Against his will, we insisted that Auggie go with us to see George's swim meet in Spencer, Iowa. When we pulled into the YMCA parking lot, our indignant passenger refused to go inside. Since it was an unusually warm February day, we reluctantly agreed to let him read a book in the parked minivan.

About an hour into the meet, Auggie appeared on the pool deck like a back-lit vision of a Renaissance saint; he seemed to glow. In his hand he held a copy of *Slaughterhouse Five* that George had recently lent him. When he spotted me in the bleachers, he broadly smiled. Smiled! After taking a seat on the torturous metal bleacher beside me, he beamed, "This is such a great book, Dad." Later that night, our family ate bland subs from the Jimmy Johns on Spencer's main street. Auggie could not stop raving about the quality of the bread. His infectious boyhood joy and optimism mysteriously restored, he monologued about a promising future.

"I'm going to get a scholarship at Harvard or Yale."

"I could be a novelist, right?"

"Maybe I could teach literature in college?"

"I'd love to teach about Kurt Vonnegut. Maybe I could write a book about him. I could do that, right?"

Our family basked in his golden, manic joyfulness through a wonderful evening until depression renewed its hold on him the following morning.

JULY 2018

The vacation that April planned in the Black Hills with her side of the family included more downs than ups. If we had been near a decent mental health facility instead of in a rented cabin under Terry Peak, we probably would have had our son committed. His suicidal ideation furiously raged for the entire week. He repeatedly begged April and me to leave him alone in the cabin while the rest of the family explored the Hills. But we kept our boy close.

Then, as if by magic, about a hundred miles into the drive back home to Iowa, the chemicals in Auggie's brain temporarily righted themselves. Unusually for Auggie, this positive change in mood accompanied a political discussion. Usually when the minivan conversation slanted toward the presidential election, I did my best to shut it down, fearing a blowup. Bernie Sanders was gearing up for another presidential run, and our oldest son, Charlie, deeply felt the Bern. Only recently, Auggie had ruthlessly decried the Vermont senator for selling out the most essential tenets of socialism. To Auggie, Bernie was a poser. But to my surprise, Auggie riffed about the utopian possibilities of a Sanders administration. Instead of the scary blowup that usually concluded most political discussions with our youngest son, Auggie surprisingly transitioned his optimism for a future Bernie administration into epiphanies regarding his own mental health.

"You know, I think my brain is lying to me," Auggie opined, with the excitement of a fresh discovery. "Life is not bad. It's good. But depression skews my perceptions. From now on, I'm going to challenge those negative thoughts when they come. I'm not going to allow depression to define me." These ideas had been communicated to him dozens of times in weekly therapy sessions in Sioux Falls, but they never landed until this drive across central South Dakota's Great Plains.

For a few precious hours, our son loved his future. That light-filled drive home sustained April and me through the long, dark months to come.

NOVEMBER 2018

Although meaningfully improved from his lowest points, the fall of Auggie's senior year remained rough. God bless the kid; he tried his best to stay out of the hospital and alive. But Auggie was paralyzed with anxiety in the face of the pile of schoolwork to make up after missing most of his junior year. When he told me that he needed to read Mitch Albom's *Tuesdays with Morrie* and then interview a family member about the questions raised in the book, I snobbishly wished the English curriculum picked a better piece of literature. But more than that, I feared the battle to come in finishing this lengthy assignment considering Auggie's current state of mind.

Both of my concerns proved unfounded. As for millions of other readers, something in Albom's popular reflection on life and mortality triggered a rush of joy in our son's mood. He knocked out the entire book in a single sitting and then vociferously raved about its wisdom. To fulfill the assignment, Auggie called up his grandpa George, my stepfather. After my parents divorced when I was in the fifth grade, my mom remarried this kindhearted and wise English professor and Episcopalian. Although it took some time, George's gentle example played a central role in the development of my faith, gracefully saving me from the allure of my biological father's devout atheism. Now, through the invisible signal of a cell phone, Grandpa George ministered to Auggie.

Enveloped by an almost rapturous glee, he cherished his grandpa's thoughtful answers to questions about life, death, and faith.

The phone call joyously wandered on for nearly an hour; I discreetly placed myself within earshot so that I could eavesdrop. As I pretended to read a book, I secretly basked in Auggie's thoughtful questions, his excitement for his grandpa's answers, his respect for his distinguished elder, and the return, however briefly, of the unadulterated zeal for life that defined his preteen years. Light cracked into the darkness once again. That burning candle illuminated our living room. If only it could stay lit.

—

The final musical number in *Next to Normal* is an uplifting power ballad entitled "Light." It follows a pivotal scene in the story in which Diana, the bipolar and depressive mom, decides to leave her husband and her family so that she can pursue her recovery alone, on her own terms, and presumably off her meds. How could such a reckless and dangerous course of action possibly be wise? Yet when well-meaning critics and naysayers understandably complain that this gushingly hopeful musical finale comes out of nowhere, I stomp them back into their holes. An anthem for my life, I need "Light" to be true.

Joyously belted by the entire cast, the following lyrics dismantle then restore me. Every. Single. Night.

> We'll find the will to find our way.
> Knowing that the darkest skies will someday see
> the sun.
> When our long night is done,
> There will be light.

Although we enjoyed some brief respite from the darkness of depression in our home, blackness ruled the skies during the time I directed *Next to Normal*. But oh, how we longed to "someday see the sun."

"Light"

Surrounded and lifted by dozens of appreciative audience members, I greet April in the theater lobby after the first time that she sees the show. Her cheeks are stained with tears. Although she knows the musical well, it still works on her. After a congratulatory hug, she leans in close to me in the crowded lobby.

"That ending," she muses. "Do you think it could be true?"

"God, I hope so," I reply.

On ECT and Rainbows

I pass the weather-beaten sign at a cruise-controlled fifty-nine miles per hour and take a few moments to process the surprising marker. The cognitive delay forces me to squeeze the brakes and finesse the steering wheel just enough to successfully round a wide corner leading to Oak Grove State Park. I used to bring the boys here when they were little and still wanted to go, even though the park was more than twenty miles away from anything else interesting to them. I sometimes drove them straight from day care as one of Daddy's spontaneous late afternoon adventures. We played Frisbee on the shoreline and tried to skip rocks on the muddy river. A few years later, we pulled out here after canoeing a small stretch of the Big Sioux River on a random summer day. Their mom dropped us off a few miles upstream and moved the car downstream to meet us at Oak Grove. Pretty sure that was the last time I was here. Must have been at least nine years ago now, or more.

If given enough time, most of us fail to see the beauty of where we live. Such visual negligence comes easily, at least for me. I've grown aesthetically cynical living in Sioux County, a prosperous and manicured prairie of corn stalks, soybeans, hog confinements, and polite Republicans. But the spontaneous detour to Oak Grove State Park temporarily restores my vision. In that inimitable prairie way, you drive through a flat field with no visible sign or hope of topographical variety, and then, like magic, the upper ridge of a previously invisible basin appears below the horizon; it dives dramatically into a verdant valley of trees, birds, deer, and picnic shelters. Like all of those unspoiled, bygone times when I drove here with my boys when they were still boys, the reveal surprises me with delight. A simple thing, but so needed now.

I only noticed the sign for Oak Grove because I chose a different route home on the daily trek back from Sioux Falls where Auggie, now seventeen years old, fumes in a locked-down hospital ward for suicidal teens. I usually take a more direct highway, but this afternoon's visit was particularly rough. My son's serotonin-starved brain locked his mood in a spiral of suicidal ideation and anger directed at loved ones. His last words to me before I left, "I hope you die in a car crash on the drive home," looped in my own brain.

Left to my own devices, I would have entertained the option of a phone call in place of these brutal daily visits, at least every once in a while. But April forbids it. More sacrificial, more unconditional than me, she insists that one of us drive the 150-mile round trip every single day. Despite his seeming inability to hear us, we must remind our beautiful boy that he is indeed loved. She is right, of course, but, man, it hurts to go—like watching a dream devolve into a nightmare. Our parental agony does not compare to Auggie's deep dread of life, of course, which somehow makes things even worse. If only we weren't so helpless; if only we could carry it for him for a while, we would. Unfortunately, depression does not work that way.

Driving by campsites, shelters, and primitive cabins at fifteen miles per hour, I descend down Oak Grove's winding road to the valley below. Dusk begins to settle into evening on this late spring Sunday, a Sabbath day. A superficial rain drips just enough moisture on the windshield to require the occasional use of my shrieking wipers, smearing bug guts across the glass. As I reach the valley's bottom—a lush oval meadow of picnic spots adjoined by a boat ramp—I notice a group of unaccompanied teenagers in a late spring revelry. Two of them tend a campfire at a designated pit, while three others giggle and rock on two colorful hammocks precariously strung from nearby trees. I resent their carefree lives and park as far away from them as I can.

I barely feel the gentle rain as I reach into the hatchback of my supercompact car—my colleagues call it the clown car—and withdraw a commemorative windbreaker that *Sports Illustrated* sent me the last time the Denver Broncos won a Super Bowl. I barely need it. I walk toward the water, overhearing the distant teenagers giggle. The river, running high this early in May, soon obscures their voices as it laps over the crumbling shoreline onto the grass. My eyes trace the braided current upstream away from the setting sun toward the forested skyline. That's when I notice the rainbow.

Almost a full rainbow, actually. It curves dramatically toward the heavens until its arching top blends into the gray-blue sky and temporarily disappears, only to be picked up again by an identical spectrum of light shooting to earth on the parallel side. How did I not see this until now? The rainbow dominates the sky. The racing river flows out of the center of the half circle of red and orange and green and blue and purple. The spectacle is magnificent and dazing.

As I marvel at the rainbow, it occurs to me that I may have read this rare but natural occurrence differently in the not-so-distant past. That was three years ago—before clinical depression visited my children; before my middle son suddenly stopped getting out of bed for school in the morning a month into his junior year; before the yelling; before the resisted therapy; before the trips to distant specialists; before the ineffective drugs that took several months to discover that they were ineffective; before the special blood tests not covered by insurance; before dropping out of swimming and band; before the cuttings; before the hospitalizations; before the $13,000 credit card balance for a hospital stay that crossed into the new fiscal year; before the cautious visits with empathic school administrators to discuss failing grades; before the experimental ketamine drug trials in other states; before the daily grind to simply live; before the constant helicopter parenting prodding the half-assed completion of late assignments required for graduation; before limping through the end of his senior year; before the attempt at college followed shortly thereafter by the medical withdrawal; before the awkward inquiries from concerned friends about how my nineteen-year-old son, previously recruited by colleges as a swimmer and honors student, now spends his days isolated in a dark basement looking at screens and professing a philosophy of angsty nihilism.

That was also before my youngest son hit this same wall of despair. Before his weekly visits to psychologists and psychiatrists in Sioux Falls who knew us so well by then that they gave us their personal email addresses; before more blood tests; before the newer drugs not covered by insurance—all ineffective; before the cuttings; before the suicide threats and attempt; before quitting cross-country, soccer, and the tuba; before the hospitalizations; before the crippling anxiety; before completely dropping out of high school five weeks before the end of his junior year; before the medical recommendation to send him to the other side of the state to a long-term facility for delinquent youth, which we refused to do; before the desperate turn to ECT (electroconvulsive therapy) that required three psychiatrists to sign off on because they'd prefer, if possible, not to zap a teenager's still-developing brain.

Before depression took control of almost every facet of our lives, I might have viewed this rainbow differently. Had it appeared during the early days of this joyless journey, I might have embraced this surprising rainbow as a sign from God that everything was going to be okay. I'm awed and appreciative, but I don't see the rainbow this way today.

We have all prayed so much these past three years. Daily petitions have humbled me and tethered me to God. More so than ever before, prayer is the rhythm of my life. Our faithful prayer chains also link dozens of pious believers over thousands of miles ceaselessly praying for our boys. But throughout this fury of depression and well-intended medical dead ends, God's role remains a mystery. Maybe things would be even worse for my boys without these intercessions, but such logic relies on proving negatives. And I've grown weary of looking for signs.

Three long years ago, I would have likely interpreted this beautiful rainbow as an assurance that the ECT treatments scheduled to start next week will provide the medical miracle necessary to allow our boy to want to live. I have prayed this multiple times today alone, but I'm wary of seeing the rainbow as an assurance of a future for Auggie.

Sign seeking seems pointless in this feckless and helpless time, this darkling plain—an existence so polluted by worry and regret that food doesn't taste as good as it used to and previous expectations of family flourishing now seem like voyeuristic pipe dreams. Something enjoyed by other families.

Don't get me wrong; I plead for healing daily, hourly. But an immutable God may have other designs. Rather than rerouting me away from this valley of the shadow of death, my pleading faith sustains me in it. I hesitate to say *through* it, because that suggests there is a way out that I can't assume. But this glorious rainbow reminds me that beauty still exists around us, and that, more than ever, I need to witness it. That's all. Perhaps God sometimes surprises us with rainbows not to signal the end of the storm, but to help us endure the storm. And that's got to be enough for today.

Brotherly Love

At six feet four with a guitar case in each hand, George makes a striking impression as he waits beside me at the final security checkpoint. A disheveled shock of thick brown hair adds an air of rugged nonchalance to his handsome features. His first attempt at college ended with a medical withdrawal over seven months ago, and he doesn't have much to dress up for these days now that he is riding out a wave of major depression at home. Guitars in hands, George patiently waits as I fumble with the keypunch intercom system in my clumsy attempt to let the attendant of this locked-down adolescent hospital ward know that Auggie's visitors have arrived.

Once through the door, I carry in Auggie's standing order of a vanilla shake from the nearby Five Guys while George follows behind by a few steps. Warned of our arrival, Auggie stands in the doorway of his little room. As soon as we reach him, he takes the vanilla shake from my hand, and I force an awkward hug. If my son is happy to see me, the oppressor who forced him here, he does a good job of hiding it. Auggie then turns his back to us and starts walking toward the windowed conference room at the far edge of the large communal space littered with depressed teenagers and their sheepish visiting parents.

Once in the conference room, George hands his little brother one of the guitars. Without talking much, they fill the next few minutes tuning their instruments by ear since this in-patient wing of the hospital does not permit cell phones with their helpful guitar apps. After adjusting the strings to near perfect harmony, George begins to strum. Auggie quickly joins in, eyes fixed upon the chord fingerings made by his older brother's left hand. For half an hour, they fill the conference room with loud and angry covers from The National, Dinosaur Jr., and Car Seat Headrest. A highlight viscerally hits when they simultaneously belt out a lyric from Car Seat Headrest's "Drunk Drivers/Killer Whales."[6] With both of their baritone voices stretched past the top of their ranges, they screech the anthem "It doesn't have to be like this" with shared conviction.

During breaks between songs, I try to talk with Auggie, to ask him about his care, to encourage him. He responds to my fumbling questions with anger and derision. Before this goes too far, sweet George preemptively strums a new chord. As if by magic, the music subsumes his brother's ire, and they play together again as one.

During this dark age in which depression rules and shapes the Hubbard home, my heart brims with gratitude for George. The burden of the disease he shares with his little brother weighs him down, putting most plans on hold. But George still finds the strength to help his younger sibling survive. In these visits, he intuitively knows what Auggie needs. With kindness and a knowing wisdom that transcends the harrowing time, brothers make music. Their rebellious, beautiful waves of sound infiltrate a little brother's screaming brain. For a short yet holy time, music mends the suffering soul.

FEBRUARY 2019

I sneak out of our bedroom toward the kitchen in hopes of finding a 9 p.m. snack. My willpower to stay away from food in the late evening vanishes during my transformation into a stressed-out fifty-year-old man. As I stalk the kitchen cupboards, I survey the full length of the main floor of our house. I see Auggie sitting at the dining room table about fifteen feet away. His huge hand—his grandfather's hand—holds up his forehead as he intently stares downward. His oldest brother, Charlie, sits beside him, close enough to read the algebra textbook open on the table under Auggie's gaze. Charlie's striking flow of red hair glistens in the dim dining-room light.

I listen, but I can barely hear what Charlie says to Auggie; he speaks in such gentle and encouraging tones. Getting Auggie to the table two hours earlier took some preternatural persuasion. Auggie viscerally fears advanced algebra and what not passing it again would mean to his hope of graduating from high school. I bribed him with encouragement, a vanilla latte, and money. But within his older brother's tender care, he now seems at peace, even confident. Charlie patiently observes him; Auggie slowly works through a proof. A born teacher, Charlie knows when to answer a question with a more helpful question. Auggie is learning despite the paralyzing fear of math, despite the dogged depression that continually lies to Auggie's brain. Somehow, Charlie's presence makes this learning possible.

Charlie doesn't even live in the house these days, but here he is. A junior math major in college, he graciously travels the six blocks from his college dorm, from his social life, from his demanding courseload, to sit beside his brother for hours at a time. Both April and I suck at math, a clear deficit of character. I gave up trying to help our kids with their math homework when fractions started multiplying. Thankfully, our gifted oldest son has always loved numbers and the logical conclusions they inspire. The summer before his freshmen year of high school, Charlie taught himself algebra with nothing but the aid of a loaned textbook so that he could pass the test that put him in the accelerated section. By his senior year of high school, military academies and engineering schools tried to recruit our math wizard after somehow gaining access to his ACT scores. Thankfully for us, Charlie chose to study math and education at the little college in our little town.

But from my unnoticed vantage spot across the house, I witness more than an older brother doling out his knowledge of advanced algebra. These two young men may not confide their thoughts and feelings in the traditional, brotherly ways. But on this winter evening, they share in something much more profound. They communicate *agapē* through an ancient, Arabic system for measuring out the world. I witness love in action via numbers and variables.

Cecil and Medea

A treasured photo reveals a lot.

This one shows Auggie holding two dogs in his lap: Cecil, a bouncy German shepherd puppy mix that George picked out from the pound four months after our beloved border collie Igor passed away, and Medea, a feisty rat terrier and unofficial therapy dog that Auggie picked out from the pound as a reward for completing an extended hospital stay for major depression. After stubbornly refusing to participate in his in-patient therapy for weeks, Auggie finally agreed to work through his program after we promised that he could have his own dog when he safely returned home.

In the photo, Medea is tensing up to bite her dreaded enemy invader in his stupid, pointy face. Cecil wants to worm his way into Auggie's prime cuddling real estate, but this pesky little bitch will not be chill. Despite Medea's omnipresent growls, this dopey, giant, German fool refuses to leave her and *her* boy alone.

The picture reveals Auggie giving and receiving love. Throughout his volatile life, one quality about our boy never altered. During the unbridled joy of his early childhood, amid the explosive mood swings of middle school, through the sinister pit of major depression that dominated high school and college, Auggie found healing comfort in the embrace of our cherished family pets. Over time, this menagerie included three dogs and one cranky cat. These creatures lavished comfort on our son through many dark nights of the soul. He considered them his best friends. When he gave up on living in the dorms during his freshman year of college, Grandma Violet wisely diagnosed, "Auggie is better off at home. He needs to be with his animals."

When the photo was taken, depression holds our son tightly in its grip, but Auggie still clings to an Old Testament vision of the new earth: a place where peace shall reign in the animal world, where "the wolf and the lamb will feed together," where "they will neither harm nor destroy / on all my holy mountain" (Isa. 65:25 NIV).

Fear, Loathing, and Caffeine Runs

During his freshman year of college, I spend nearly every moment of the day wondering how Auggie is doing, hoping for the best, fearing the worst.

He completely gave up on living in the dorms two weeks ago and moved back home. But he's *not* at home when I walk into the house at six thirty on this frigid Tuesday evening in early November. I check his room; I check the basement; nothing. He usually walks home after band practice finishes in late afternoon, but he is nowhere to be found. I had a production meeting today. I should have come home first or skipped the damn meeting, God help me. I text him but receive no response. *Dear Lord*, I pray. *Please let my boy be okay.*

An hour passes and Auggie still has not responded to my texts. I'm freaking out. At seven thirty I put on my winter coat and leave the house to search for our college freshman in the usual places. Trying to be optimistic, I first search in the spots where he would be most unlikely to notice my texts, starting with the music building. I linger for a time in the hallway, but no melancholy tuba sounds escape through the practice-room doors. Next, I walk over to the Rec Center. Auggie sometimes tries to outrun his depression on the treadmill, an occasionally effective therapy if he can muster the energy to get started. He's not there either, so I head to the library.

I plan to check the study carrels first, a secluded column of tiny rooms on the far side of the second floor that he likes to hide out in. To my surprise, however, I spot him the moment I enter the building sitting in a low-slung lounger near the library's entrance. His eyes are clenched closed, his headphones in, his body twisted forward in what looks like misery.

"Auggie?" I whisper, my volume automatically in library mode. No answer. His music is too loud.

"Auggie?" I ask again, this time gently touching his shoulder. When his eyes flash open, the blazing wild blue fury within them immediately signals things are not going well. He yanks his headphones out of his ears.

"I can't," he mumbles. "The FYS paper is due tomorrow, and I can't do it. It's such a stupid paper. 'This I Believe?' What a joke. Who cares what I believe? It's ridiculous."

Since I am currently teaching another section of this same class, I know exactly what he's referring to.

"It's not so bad," I gently counter. "Let me help you. All you have to do is tell a story from your life and then reflect on what you learned from the experience. And hey, it's just the draft that's due. We can knock it out in a couple of hours, tops."

In response, he clenches his jaw and bares his teeth in a way that the rest of the animal kingdom would surely interpret as a snarl. His entire body curls as if in resistance. But then, with a deep, dramatic sigh, he leans forward and unzips his absurdly overstuffed college backpack. A distant observer might deduce that his laptop computer weighs two hundred pounds based on the effort it seems to take him to withdraw it from the backpack's protective sleeve.

"Let me get you a vanilla latte first," I pronounce.

We first noticed when Auggie was a senior in high school that a shot of caffeine often miraculously pulled him out of a hopeless mood. We learned this treatment by sheer accident. Just minutes after drinking coffee, the dark cloud often lifted. While sadly limited to a few hours of respite, a strong caffeinated beverage salvaged many evenings for our boy. Nights were always the worst. To avoid latte runs to our local coffee shop before evening events or study sessions, we bought him his own Keurig for his now-abandoned dorm room. His skeptical psychiatrist offered no explanation for caffeine's restorative effect. Officially diagnosed as medication resistant, our long-suffering son has tested every major family of antidepressant over the past four and a half years of treatment with no noticeable effect other than weight gain from Zoloft. We stick to the regimen of pharmaceuticals, of course, in the increasingly distant hope that one of them may eventually work. In the meantime, I gladly buy Auggie as many vanilla lattes as he needs.

I lug his large, base-drum-sized latte from the library coffee kiosk and set it on the little table beside his low-slung chair. He stares angrily at the assignment description on his computer screen between cautious sips of the hot beverage. The next twenty minutes are rough.

"It's embarrassing and dumb to force me to write about myself. Other students are going to read this."

"I don't know. The autobiographical essay has a long tradition, and you have some amazing stories."

"How is writing a story about myself going to be helpful in the real world?"

"It's good practice to develop your writing skills."

"It's pretentious to imply that people could learn something important from one of my stories."

"I disagree. Seeing how hard you work and how far you've come with your depression might give others hope."

"Maybe . . ."

As the caffeine finally starts to kick in, his sour mood slowly mellows.

"Maybe I'll write about how I dropped out of high school for a while, and how I didn't think I'd ever finish. But then they gave me extra time in study hall, and worked with me, and I was able to make up the missed work during my senior year. Even the math."

"That sounds promising. It would be best if you could pick something specific from that time and focus on it. Maybe you could write about how you ended up getting an A in advanced algebra your last semester of high school after dropping out of it your junior year?"

"But what could I say I learned from that? I mean, this paper is called 'This I Believe,' right?"

"Remember when you won that award for resilience at the senior assembly? That was a great day."

—

Over three hours later, just before midnight, Auggie and I finally leave the library together for home and bed. Although I helped him proof his paper, he required little assistance writing it. Exhausted, I even tried to get him to call it a night two hours in, but he persisted. Like many other times in his short college career, Auggie started slow, found his stride, then refused to stop. Although a sloppy draft easily would have sufficed for this early stage of the assignment, he would have none of it. He insisted on carefully rewriting and editing his essay until it said what he wanted it to say in the way he wanted to say it, until it said what he truly believed.

For me, this evening began in fear; for Auggie, it began with loathing. But as the cool midnight November air nips our cheeks outside of the library doors, I give silent thanks for the gift that this evening has become, to help my boy, to sit beside him for hours, to bask in his fierce intensity and hard-earned wisdom.

A Midsummer Night's Dream in October

How many times have I made this drive? I lost count years ago.

In the past two decades, three different minivans wore themselves out on the straight, expansive highways linking Iowa and North Dakota. Initially, we braved this trek with car seats filled with babbling toddlers; later, elementary-school-aged boys passed the hours watching cartoons on a tiny TV with a built-in VHS player that I plugged into the minivan's old-school cigarette lighter and precariously strapped into the gap between the two front seats with a bungee cord; on subsequent journeys, teenagers whiled away the time with carefully negotiated mixtures of books and handheld video games. At April's insistence, these eight-hour treks took place six times each year, or more. "The kids need to know their grandparents," she would rightly say. "This is, after all, the main reason we moved back closer to home." By the standards of the Great Plains, what's a measly five hundred miles?

In the year and a half since April accepted a college teaching gig near her hometown in North Dakota, these daylong commutes have only increased in frequency. April and I try to see each other once a month until summer finally reunites us. With our kids now grown, I usually drive the 482 miles to see my wife alone, but thankfully today is wonderfully different. As I aim the steering wheel due north, Auggie sits beside me in the minivan's passenger seat. Through serendipity, April's fall production of Shakespeare's *A Midsummer Night's Dream* coincides with our college midterm break; Auggie and I both have two extra days off. I did not have to twist his arm to come with me; our boy truly wants to see his mom and her show. Turnabout is fair play. Just two weeks ago, April drove the same stretch of lonely road to Iowa to witness Auggie act in a Shakespeare play that I directed.

Even though he started college as a music major, Auggie tried out for plays during his freshman year. He did not get cast his first semester, but a theatre colleague eventually put him into the winter musical: the Steve Martin and Edie Brickell bluegrass fable *Bright Star*. Unfortunately, a massive new wave of depression and anxiety collided with the production. As always, evenings in the winter were the worst. Although his booming baritone voice served the musical well, Auggie barely made it through the late-night rehearsals and performances. One evening, I received a frantic phone call from backstage, "I can't do it, Dad. I am not safe." I rushed to the theater and ended up telling the sympathetic director that Auggie wasn't up for it that night; we left the rehearsal together early. He managed to come back and eventually finished the show. Two days after *Bright Star* closed in February 2019, Auggie withdrew from college for the rest of the spring semester.

When he returned in the fall, Auggie fought so hard for his passions, for his mental health, for his education, for his future. He auditioned for theatre again and earned the supporting role of love-sick Longaville in my fall production of Shakespeare's *Love's Labour's Lost*. As in the past, Auggie struggled with anxiety and connecting socially within the tight-knit cast, but he pressed on. A student of his moods, I learned to be careful giving him notes, especially after a long evening rehearsal.

A resilient memory from this optimistic time often visits me. It took place on a brisk October Iowa evening after a dress rehearsal run-through in Windmill Park, our outdoor COVID accommodation. I had just finished giving notes to the rest of the cast but held back on Auggie's because I feared overwhelming my depleted son. As the ensemble dispersed to pack things up and trek the six blocks back to campus, Auggie tentatively approached me near the cement lip of the bandshell's stage.

"Am I doing okay in the show, Dad?" he asked, concerned.

"You are doing so well," I replied. "I have a few notes that I'll give you tomorrow. Please know that I'm so proud of you."

To assure him, I leaned in to hug my boy. He leaned in too. We held each other for a much longer time than I expected.

—

The backseat of the minivan holds two unruly additional passengers: much-loved dogs who cannot be left alone. Cecil, our odd and handsome German shepherd mix, sleeps for most the trip. Medea, Auggie's feisty rat terrier, continually expresses her discontent during the stretches of the drive in which she's not permitted to press her boney little body into Auggie's lap. Since Auggie never got his license, he cannot help with the driving, but he contributes mightily by taking care of the captive dogs. We fill the miles with bright conversations about possible majors, college classes, and the prospects that the slumping Denver Broncos may one day win another football game.

Not every long-distance drive with Auggie is this sweet. Last spring, shortly after his medical withdrawal from college due to a flare-up of depression, he fumed beside me along this same stretch of interstate highway. His difficult yet necessary decision to postpone his education only fueled his self-loathing, despair, and paranoia. As the miles lagged on, Auggie struggled to endure my futile attempts at friendly small talk and repeatedly accused me of putting bad things into his food. He stopped taking care of the dogs. Somewhere in South Dakota on the drive back home, we hit a low point.

To stay awake on long drives, I often listen to National Public Radio. When I stupidly sided with an NPR commentator who questioned China's handling of the COVID crisis, Auggie, his collectivist ideology challenged, flew into a screaming rage. My depressed son lashed out at me in a seething, vitriolic, and profane explosion of angry shouts. I tried to de-escalate the conflict by refusing to respond to his pointed, screaming questions about communism's superior health-care systems. But I was too late. My unwelcome silence only infuriated Auggie more. While shouting angry questions, he wrongly interpreted my clenched jaw as a pretentious smirk. As we shot down Interstate 29 at eighty miles per hour, Auggie spontaneously slugged me hard on the passenger side of my head. Although my ear rang like a gong, I somehow kept the car on the road. Instantly stricken with shame and guilt, Auggie profusely apologized, after which he fell into a near catatonic state. He slept for the rest of the drive.

But today is different. Today, the October morning and midday hours fly by in bouncy conversation scored by mutually agreed upon musical selections. During one stretch, we play all three Mumford and Sons albums back-to-back-to-back. Tired yet ripe with optimism, we finally pull into the parking lot of Lake Region State College in Devils Lake shortly after 5 p.m. No matter how hard I try, I cannot make the drive in under eight hours. The lights go up on *A Midsummer Night's Dream* in about two hours, so I failed to arrive in time to drop the dogs off at the family farm before dinner and the show. To compensate, Auggie helpfully guides the rambunctious canines to a nearby green patch to pee as I text April to let her know we have arrived. Thrilled to see her youngest boy and her man, April bursts out of her office-building door. A sweet reunion transpires as Auggie, I, and two attention-greedy pups reunite with the matriarch in the community college parking lot. It was only the beginning of a magical evening.

After enjoying a meal together at the finest restaurant that Devils Lake has to offer, we return to campus after dusk in time to witness *A Midsummer Night's Dream*. Auggie conscientiously makes sure the dogs have water before packing them into the minivan on this cool October evening. Once inside the theater, the new COVID guidelines prove easy to follow with only twenty audience members in attendance. Since April needs to run the lights, Auggie and I search for two seats in the three-hundred-seat auditorium. To ensure a good view and to visually support the actors, we decide to sit in the front row of the large, mostly empty house.

For the next ninety minutes, April's artful, masked production of Shakespeare's classic comic romp takes the stage, masterfully cut to be performed by a cast of only six actors. COVID protocols inspired April to make several creative directorial choices. With each inventive decision, I glance sideways at Auggie. Even through his mask, I sense his broad, proud smile. Near the end of the performance, when the rude mechanicals histrionically perform the lamentable tragedy of Pyramus and Thisbe, Auggie dissolves into delighted giggles. The child of theatre professors, he knows how to appreciate his mom's imaginative use of open-focus staging to safely bring Shakespeare's hysterical metaplay to new life. When the lights come up for the curtain call, Auggie immediately rises to his feet. In this timid, tiny crowd, he is the only one. I pop up beside him, and we clap together in solidarity as the actors take their grateful bows.

"You did a very good job with the play, Mom," Auggie offers with deep sincerity after seeking out his mom in the theater lobby. "That was an excellent show."

In my heart I know that this broad praise for the fruits of his mother's vocation only expresses the tip of Auggie's admiration and advocacy. As a young boy, Auggie witnessed his mom take the helm of dozens of theatrical productions, including well-funded and large-cast musicals such as *The Secret Garden* and *Urinetown*— the latter broke all attendance records at the nearby Christian college where she taught. Unfortunately, the parodic content of this silly show prickled the humorless ire of a gatekeeping administration who bizarrely feared this wonderful woman's influence upon their covenant youth. Eventually and painfully, April resigned from that ungrateful and inhospitable place.

For the next six years, Auggie witnessed his resourceful mom scramble to make art anywhere she could on the underpopulated prairie, from community theatre to summer stock, from an extended gig at the college where I teach to a January-term guest-directing slot at a college in another state. Unfortunately, even though successful, these productions ultimately proved transitory in the fleeting, fickle, ephemeral world of live theatre. So, when his mom reported in the late summer of 2019 that a small state college near her hometown in North Dakota had recruited her to be their theatre professor, Auggie immediately piped up, "That is great. You have to take that, Mom!" April never would have taken the job if he had asked her to stay.

Auggie knew he would miss his mom, of course; throughout his long battles with depression, April's empathy and intuition served him better than my cold attempts to problem-solve; he fully understood that the distance from his great understander may be rough. Nonetheless, a loving son resolutely encouraged his beloved mother. He wanted the most important woman in his life to once again be properly paid to do the thing she loved. Above all else, he wanted her to thrive and flourish once more as a professional theatre artist and teacher. He was proud of her.

Actors use the term "subtext" to express the deeper meaning underscoring bits of dialogue within a play. In the spirit of this theatrical convention, Auggie's compliment, "You did a very good job with this play, Mom," inwardly meant so much more than simple kind words outwardly expressed.

—

Many years ago, we discovered an oasis near the halfway point of the drive between Edmore, North Dakota, and Orange City, Iowa. This convenient South Dakota rest-stop refuge sits near the intersection of Interstate 29 and Highway 12—the passageway to Aberdeen by way of Waubay, if for some reason you ever wanted to veer west. We started strategically timing our fueling stops here when we realized that this large Coffee Cup Fuel Stop conglomeration of retail services included a genuine Caribou Coffee shop hidden in its midst. Time after time, as our minivans filled up with gas, we went inside and filled our travel cups with decent caffeinated beverages, so much better than the truck-stop swill brewed just feet away. Our oasis also included other incentives that kept us dropping by. The best of these by far—better than the booths for Pizza Hut or Cinnabon, more helpful than the wide assortment of deep-fried cheese curds or trucker-appropriate leather goods, more inviting than the kiosk for the Prairie Berry Winery that sold a vintage vino called Red Ass Rhubarb—better than all these roadside attractions was the fenced dog park connected to the truck-stop parking lot. In a much-needed service to people like us who regularly travel with their dogs, this patch of poop-filled prairie stole a small swath of the endless Great Plains for pups to pee, poop, and frolic.

It's Sunday afternoon on the drive back from our idyllic October midsummer night's dream in North Dakota. The difficulty of saying good-bye to April caused a late start, and I am now trying to turn the minivan into a time machine since college resumes tomorrow morning. And the weather is turning bad. With nothing to stop it, the bitter, potent prairie wind cuts through our light fall jackets and causes our uncovered hands to quickly numb whenever we exit the heated minivan. Per our arrangement, I pump the gas before going into the truck stop to purchase a dark roast coffee for myself and a vanilla latte for Auggie at the Caribou Coffee stand. While I do my part, Auggie leashes both dogs and, with gentle tugs, guides their restless energy to the fenced dog park thirty yards or so from the pumping gas.

When I finally return to the topped-off minivan with our caffeinated beverages warming both my hands, I notice Auggie still standing in the dog park at the far north edge of the parking lot. I settle our coffee in the drink holders and drive the short distance to the fenced enclosure. With his hands pressed into his pockets against the frigid wind, Auggie stoically stands near the center of the dog park; his neurotic and freezing rat terrier trembles near his ankles. Auggie must be freezing too, but he does not move toward the heated minivan when I arrive. Instead, he lovingly watches our German shepherd, Cecil, obsessively sniff the ground. Although the dog must need to pee like a racehorse, Cecil proves incapable of relaxing his anxious bladder. There is just too darn much pee and poop to smell for him to pee himself.

If I were in Auggie's place, as I have been several times before, I would have lost my temper by this point and forced my irritating dog back into the car even with his bladder full. Auggie, however, does not scold or cajole the transfixed German shepherd. With no complaint, he withstands the bitter wind and patiently waits for his beloved charge to take care of business.

His strong jaw juts out in what might have been a smirking grimace inspired by the cold. But I recall his etched expression as a loving smile.

The Mourning Tuba

The early days of the COVID lockdown crawl by at a fearful, lethargic pace. When my college finally went fully online, faculty were initially told to stay away from campus, lest we infect the essential workers. So, the fact that the conductor of the college band graciously helps me and Auggie check out a tuba from the sealed-off instrument-storage room represents an act of both kindness and bravery.

Under her direction, Auggie drags the massive instrument from the stuffy, enclosed storage room, a place of perceived danger, into the safer open air of the music-building parking lot. Before we may load the encased tuba into our waiting minivan, the conductor must first conduct an instrument inspection. This is before we knew enough to wear masks, so I watch from what I guess is a safe distance as Auggie holds the bulky case open on the parking-lot asphalt in the blustery winds of early March.

As the conductor crouches to test the tuba's valves, a nearby voice commands, "Not so close. Auggie, please step back from Dr. Holt while she's doing that." The voice comes from another music professor, a kind advocate for Auggie, who happens to be on her way to smuggle a needed book out of her locked-down office suite. The fear we live with during these bizarro times is new and strange. But for the Hubbard clan, these new pandemic anxieties pale against the nightmare of living with clinical depression these past four years.

Auggie has not touched a tuba in three months. After success-fully completing the fall semester of his freshman year of college, he abruptly dropped his music major along with all music courses, including band. He started the spring semester like gangbusters, intent on saving the world as a sociology major. But then depres-sion renewed its sinister grip, and he had to take a medical with-drawal halfway through the spring term. Two weeks after Auggie withdrew, COVID sent everyone else home too.

Sequestered from this upside-down and unreliable world, one thing became clear to our youngest child: Auggie needed more music in his life. I emailed his former band conductor and, with Auggie's enthusiastic consent, negotiated a gracious bargain. We could rent a tuba for the spring and summer, provided Auggie promised to play in the band again when students hopefully re-turned to in-person learning in the fall. Tuba players, especially good ones, are worth their weight in brass to conductors of small college bands. "No matter what I major in," Auggie promised, "from now on, I'm always going to play my tuba."

And so he did.

From that day forward throughout the lockdown, Auggie prac-ticed for at least an hour every single day. A devotee of prescribed routines, he always started each rehearsal by playing a series of whole-note progressions, working on breath support and tone. This simple warm-up ritual lasted twenty minutes or more. April and I rejoiced to hear these mellow, gentle booms return to our home. If art holds a mirror up to nature, Auggie's sorrowful tuba warm-ups reflected the sadness of a globe without human interaction. More-over, the mournful whole notes, so masterfully held, reverberated the unending melancholia that plagued the long-suffering player. While somber, nothing wallowing or self-indulgent escaped into Auggie's musical interpretation. With elegant understatement, our talented son made clear through his tuba what words failed to express. In euphonious prayers of lament, Auggie transformed despair into subtle beauty.

When classes resumed that fall, Auggie took his promised place holding down the low brass section of his college band. He also earned work-study money by playing for the pep band at football games. In addition to band rehearsals, his meticulous routine included daily visits to the music-building practice rooms. No doubt you would have heard the resounding sound of his whole notes if you happened to walk by. That fall semester, his mourning tuba wove into the playlist of the music-building soundtrack. At various points, bystanders—music students or fellow professors—reported back to me what their eavesdropping ears had witnessed in the hallway near his preferred practice room. These kind, unsolicited reports usually included versions of the phrases: "Auggie has such a beautiful tone," or "Auggie can make that tuba weep."

Since before his junior year of high school, April and I had discussed buying our musical son his own tuba—not a minor purchase for us. Even a good *used* tuba costs $10,000 or more. We came close his freshman year of college, visiting websites and talking with experts, but then Auggie abruptly dropped his music major. When he returned to playing during the spring of 2020, we resolved to use the extra money that April earned from working in North Dakota to finally buy our boy a proper horn. My to-do list for the third week of October of 2020 included the item: "Make appointment at the bank with a loan officer about buying Auggie a tuba."

I wish I had hurried.

Majors

I'm going to be the next Øystein Baadsvik; he's the best tuba player in the world. Can I do that with a music major from Northwestern?"

"I'm going to major in psychology and go on to get a PhD; do you think I should also get a minor in biochemistry? That seems to be the way all the best research in psychology is heading."

"If I major in sociology, could I become a community organizer? That would be the best way to enact positive social change, right?"

"What math classes do I need for a major in economics? Because I'll need a strong background in economics to write the definitive book proving that capitalism is a failed system."

"Why did they cut the literature track from the English major? So stupid! I was thinking of majoring in literature; what is the Vice President of Academic Affairs' email so I can complain?"

"How can a liberal arts college cut its philosophy major? Philosophy is the only major, really, if you think about it; all other majors track back to philosophy, right?"

"History would be a pretty cool major, but I don't want to teach. Maybe I could write for a think tank?"

"Should I register for Greek or Hebrew in the fall? I'll need them both if I decide to major in biblical and theological studies."

"Political science has the coolest classes, I think, but I'm worried that the faculty don't properly understand the principles of Marxism."

"I'm going to declare as a theatre major, Dad. I could do lots of cool things with a theatre major, right?"

—

For over a year, the dilemma of choosing a major in college dominates nearly every conversation we have with Auggie. He can't decide. Leaflets of crumpled propaganda from every department on campus insulate the bottom of his overstuffed backpack. He's interested in everything.

Auggie starts his freshmen year as a music major. He loves the theory and performing in three different ensembles. His fellow music majors marvel at how he practices more than any other player in the band. For his first juried recital, his tuba instructor assigns a piece of music meant to be played on a smaller-sized tuba than the one we rent from the Music Department. Although he practices countless hours, Auggie fails to clearly hit the highest notes of the prescribed sonata. Hating that he did not sound perfect in front of his peers, he immediately drops all the music classes that he is registered for in the spring. "I'm never going to be good enough to be a professional tuba player," he reasons. "Besides, how would playing in an elitist orchestra help the global poor?"

As the spring semester begins, Auggie enrolls in courses in sociology and psychology, vacillating between the two as majors. But before he can decide, a fierce new wave of depression grips him and forces the midsemester medical withdrawal. Once unenrolled, he immediately laments that he is not taking any classes and revs up his major speculation obsession to new heights. "Can I take summer classes?" he begs. Auggie enrolls in online summer courses in religion and psychology. He falls in love with both, of course, as new insights bounce around and feed his curious brain. He earns an A in both classes.

Auggie is full of anticipation and hope as the fall semester finally starts, with a new set of possibilities. His much-altered course schedule now includes my intro course in theatre, a general education credit. He pores over the required texts and, before the semester even begins, proudly announces to the world that he is now a theatre major.

I have mixed feelings about this development. I'd love to share more of my field with him, but I wonder if theatre fits Auggie's complicated set of predispositions. Because of his autism, he dislikes small group settings, a requisite of theatre. And although he has been onstage many times growing up—a hazard of having theatre professors for parents—Auggie genuinely appears uncomfortable acting, at least to me. With so many interests, I wonder if our son might be better suited for a less socially rigorous major such as music, psychology, or history. I suspect that an unexamined desire to please his theatre-professor parents is at the root of this newest choice of major. So, mindful not to hurt his feelings, I gently suggest alternative subjects that might better suit our son's unique combination of gifts and passions.

But then I experience the glorious joy of Auggie as a student in my class.

To reason with the thickheaded Nazarenes, King James's Jesus laments, "Verily I say unto you, no prophet is accepted in his own country." For the first time, I now get to know Auggie not only as my son, with all the baggage that entails, but also as a citizen in my exclusive academic commonwealth. This kid vociferously reads and rereads every text on the syllabus. At the start of each semester, I typically ask my students to jot down questions they have about the assigned readings to discuss at the start of the next class, but few ever do. From the second day onward, our little theatre learning-community falls into a rhythm of starting each class with a list of Auggie's carefully prepared and penetrating inquiries into the readings.

After wading beside him through Aristotle's *Poetics*, through Willy Loman's modern tragic spirit, through Aristophanes's political satire, and into Strindberg's brutal naturalism, I finally fully realize how fucking brilliant this young man is. Three times a week

I gratefully witness an articulate, inquisitive, intense young student with an intellect seemingly expanding by the day.

Yes, he can be a little irritating. He was born with his hand up, so I must make a rule that Auggie is only allowed to answer every other question in the hopes that his classmates might also occasionally chime in. One day, as I listen to him carefully unpack the knotty nuances surrounding the role of social justice in William Wells Brown's nineteenth-century melodrama *The Escape: A Leap to Freedom*, a piercing observation nearly strikes me down: if I had no history with this round-faced nineteen-year-old virtuoso, and he simply showed up in a general education class I was teaching, I would surely recruit the hell out of him to consider a major in theatre. As I have publicly professed countless times, the multitudinous field of theatre extends far beyond a simple aptitude for acting. If cultivated, I truly believe Auggie's passion and intellect could shape the field for years to come.

It took eight weeks for me to fully understand that, when it came to Auggie's prophetic voice, I had played the obtuse Nazarene to the prophet in my home.

I need to find a way to tell him how gifted I think he is, but I struggle with the method. The national skepticism regarding the virtues of the life of the mind currently makes pursuing a PhD in the arts and humanities a perilous vocational pilgrimage within our culturally stultified country. And I suspect that my encouragement would likely push Auggie down this difficult path. So, I'm cautious. But I owe him the truth. He deserves to know my professional opinion as if he were not my son.

But he is my son. And our time ran out.

ACT III

The Life After

The Sounds of the Women Who Loved Auggie

I am the one who found him.

He did not show up for my 11:50 a.m. theatre class midway through the fall semester of his sophomore year. That day, we were watching a musical that the students had picked—Mel Brooks's *The Producers*. When Auggie did not show up for class, I was concerned. Phone records indicate that I texted him twice and called him once before I started teaching. He had only missed one class before. That time, after I finished teaching, I fearfully walked the short distance from the classroom to his college dorm room and found him deep in sleep. Otherwise, he never missed my class.

When the video concluded at the end of the class, I mumbled a few cryptic instructions to the students and left the room, leaving the DVD in the player, I'm told, as if that matters. I did not have to wait this time for a student to let me in the main entrance of the locked dormitory. As I trotted up the steps taking three at a time, I prayed again that he would be okay, prayed that he was just asleep, prayed as I had so many times before, prayers that always seemed to be answered, but not today. His door was unlocked.

The coroner, a local physician who happens to be the father of Auggie's greatest Accelerated Reader rival back in the glory days of fifth grade, eventually reported that August Robert Hubbard likely died between midnight and 2 a.m. the morning of October 23, 2020, at least ten hours before I found him.

I am the one who found him.

It took hours, what happened next. People came: a policeman, the chaplain, the Dean of Student Life, the Vice President of Academic Affairs, the coroner, two colleagues, and finally, the local funeral director. There may have been others. I remember people offering me a chair, a bottle of water; I don't think I took either. I remember taking off my face mask; nobody asked me to put it back on. I may have signed something. I may have answered questions from the police. People may have prayed beside me in the hallway. I'm not sure; I stood there for hours. I remember deciding not to call April, who was in North Dakota. I remember people asking me if I had called April yet. I may have wondered how they could not understand that such a conversation required privacy, and I could not possibly leave my post, my boy, until they took him away.

As the hours passed, as the news probably spread, I remember fearing that someone else might call April. That would be terrible, but still I waited. I waited until the two policeman and the funeral director finally wheeled the long stretcher out of his third-floor dorm room; a tightly fitting shroud completely covered his body. I remember watching as they twisted the stretcher down the narrow stairwell. I remember following them down three stories. I remember them tugging, and shifting, and planning at each landing as if they were professional movers trying not to scratch an expensive piece of furniture; I may have even offered to help. I remember walking beside the stretcher as it was wheeled down the entire length of the first floor dorm hallway because the funeral director decided it could not make the corner of the nearest exit; I remember curious college students standing near their open dorm-room doors trying to inconspicuously sneak a look.

I remember walking near the lobby where I'm told Auggie sometimes played his guitar and sang songs at comically high volumes; I remember exiting the dorm into the rear parking lot and then walking on the sidewalk for the entire length of the building to where the hearse sat three stories directly under Auggie's dorm-room window. I remember the funeral director opening the rear door of the hearse. I remember them lifting the stretcher so that they could collapse its legs. At this point, I asked them to stop.

"Which side is his head on," I asked.

The funeral director, skilled from decades of awkward conversations, discreetly pointed to the side nearest to the entrance of the hearse. "This side," he responded. With an audience that Auggie surely would have hated, I remember laying my body across the shroud, my head near where they told me his head was. I said something to my boy, but I don't remember what.

They loaded him in the hearse, and I watched them drive away.

Somebody, maybe a policeman, asked, "Do you need a ride?" I remember telling him that I needed to walk. He didn't argue with me.

Neuroscientists have gotten pretty good at understanding why we remember certain things and forget others. Looking back, I am surprised by how many incidences from that devastating day I cannot recall with clarity. "Shock" probably explains some of these omissions. But despite the fog of shock, neuronal spikes in my hippocampus and my amygdala must have perfectly lined up with my

theta clock on at least two occasions that awful late October afternoon; I remember both with vivid, piercing, haunting detail. First,
I remember the precise moment I found him, every agonizing detail.
I initially tried to put my first ninety seconds in his dorm room onto
this page, but the words refused to come; I now understand that this
intimate scene with my son should remain between him and me.

Second, I remember the sounds the women who loved Auggie
made when they first heard the news.

—

Finally clear of the college campus and stumbling toward my
home, I scroll to the favorites tab on my phone and touch the top
number. April does not pick up. Her mom, I think. Her mom will
need to drive forty minutes to Devils Lake to take April back to
the family farm where she lives during the school year for work.
With fingers slow from the crisp fall air, I scroll through my con-
tacts list and call my mother-in-law.

"Violet? This is Bob. I have some terrible news."

After I tell her, a long pause follows. Then I witness through
the phone this stoic, Scandinavian saint of a woman uncontrollably
weep. Through her sobs, she repeats, "Oh, no. Oh, no. Oh, Auggie.
Oh, no," at a louder volume than I have ever heard her use.

I fail to break in multiple times until my gentle pleading finally
gets her to stop long enough for me to tell her that April doesn't
know yet. That she must start driving now because her daughter
forty miles away will need her very soon. Still sobbing so loudly that
I must hold the phone slightly away from my ear, she agrees.

I try April again. No answer.

I click on Charlie's phone number. He's teaching high school
right now, but to my surprise he picks up.

"Yes, Dad?"

"I have some terrible news. There is no way to soften this. We
lost your little brother today."

"What do you mean?" he replies, fearing the euphemism.

"We lost him. He killed himself in his dorm room."

"Auggie?" He tenderly questions.

Oh, dear God, I should have clarified. We've been living with the specter of depression for so long in our afflicted family that Charlie honestly does not know which younger brother he lost. As I clarify, my phone buzzes. It is April. "I'm sorry, Charlie. Mom is on the other line. I have to take it."

"Abbey and I will be there as soon as we can," he tells me right before I hang up.

Feeling the unbearable weight of my failure to protect our son, I tap the button to pick up April's call.

"What's up my love? You called?" April so innocently asks, her mood bouncy and fun.

I draw a breath. "Are you sitting down?" I ask, like they do in the movies.

"Why?" she asks.

"You should sit down," I request.

"Yes. What is it?"

"We lost him. We lost Auggie. He's gone. I'm so sorr . . ." Her primal scream rips through the phone connection and reaches deep into the darkest places of human existence. No discernible words, only desperate, wounded screams, like an animal stuck in a bone-crushing trap, but worse. I listen, helpless. Eventually, I try to break in, to explain, but the screams persist. I hear objects breaking on the other side of the call. Finally, I hear one word, belted with deep ferocity: "How?!"

I try to explain, but the primitive and furious screams take over again. I stand in the gutter of an Orange City street littered with crunchy dead leaves and bear witness to her anguish. Finally, a strange female voice questions, "Is this April's husband?"

"Yes," I answer.

"What has happened?"

"Our son killed himself."

"Oh. Okay. We will take care of her here. She will call you back when she is able, okay?"

The call ends.

I learned later that April's cries caused all work to cease in the wing of the college where her office sits. The woman I talked to had just abandoned her biology class midlecture to see if she could help.

Next, I call George. I catch him standing at a bus stop in St. Paul, where he is now back in college. I ask him if he is with anyone. He says he is with a friend. I take a breath and reluctantly share the news with my clinically depressed middle child; I think I hear a loud thump, but he assures me it was nothing. After stumbling through some details, George promises me that he is safe, that he will stay with his friend. I promise that I will find a way to get him home as soon as possible. When I see him the next day, George's hand is swollen from smashing it against a wall the moment after he heard the news.

I then make the final call to my parents—Auggie had no bigger advocates than them; neither picks up. I leave a cryptic message on my mom's phone and hang up to finish my walk home. My remaining reserves must now be spent overseeing the many logistical duties of death that fall upon the living.

Later that evening, after more painful calls to April and my boys, I sit alone in my empty house waiting for my dispersed family to find their ways back home. My mom calls me.

"What is it, Bob? Your message was strange."

I share the news with my elderly mother, the third woman I talked to this evening who loves Auggie. She loves him with all the untamed passion of her Slovenian, barbarian tribe. Like Violet and April, my mom also responds with uncontrollable, inconsolable cries. At least thirty seconds of heartbreaking weeping passes. Eventually, my stepdad takes the phone and tells me that they will call me back when they can.

Last Rites

The funeral director offers to take control of my cell phone. In my diminished condition, I cannot seem to hold open the Book of Common Prayer (BCP) and simultaneously stream the Last Rites ceremony to April in North Dakota. This unassuming middle-aged man gently removes the phone from my trembling fingers and, with a photographer's eye, aims the camera. Through the cell phone's speaker, I hear April cry out when the image comes into view 482 miles away. The funeral director must have successfully framed the FaceTime feed to include the retired religion professor as she stands beside the cold metal table that holds the body of our youngest son. "Oh, Auggie. My boy," April gently weeps. The retired professor then performs the litany commonly known as Last Rites, the familiar red book open in her hands. As April watches virtually, two other members of our little church community, also fellow professors, bear witness in this cramped and sterile mortuary hidden in the basement of the local funeral home.

Maybe five hours have passed since I found Auggie in his dorm room. An hour ago, I received a call from our Episcopal priest. Among other tender things, she asked if I wanted Last Rites to be performed. I said yes, although I did not really understand what she was offering. Because of her immunocompromised husband, our priest cannot leave her house during this early phase of the

COVID pandemic, so she asked the retired religion professor, an ordained minister in the Reformed Church of America and a rebel member of our tiny Episcopal congregation, to conduct the short ceremony. Our priest must have also asked these two kind friends from church who stand beside me now to participate in the litany, an appropriate invitation since all three guests knew, accepted, and loved Auggie.

I tried to delay this impromptu ceremony until April could attend in person, but she will not arrive from North Dakota until tomorrow. In what strikes my shell-shocked brain as bureaucratic folly, Auggie's body must be shipped to Sioux Falls shortly. They are holding things up for us as it is, they say. Apparently, suicide requires an official inquest. Because it's Friday, the inquest will not even take place until Monday at the earliest, but Auggie's body must still be taken to the nearest properly equipped lab no later than tonight. His mom will not get to see him in person, to say good-bye, before the pathologists do their work.

Because of the inquest, the funeral director cannot do anything to soften Auggie's appearance. Through FaceTime and in person, we see him as he last was. This intimate, informal display must take place in this basement mortuary because the main floor of the funeral home is currently occupied by a prescheduled family viewing. Indeed, when I stood outside the basement door a few minutes ago waiting to be let in, I noticed nameless, grieving relatives congregating in the parking lot. I wonder if, through their grief, they gave a thought to the ragtag crew descending the steps into the normally off-limits basement of the funeral home.

—

For someone drawn to the poetry and history of liturgy, the Book of Common Prayer remains a remarkable collection. Since becoming an Episcopalian as a teenager, I have often skimmed the BCP looking for formal prayers for special occasions or trying to locate a foundational church document. Even so, I cannot recall ever noticing the following litany during my earlier pursuits. I also have no memory of saying any of the words printed below on that dreadful day of death. I do, however, vaguely recall that the ceremony, while macabre and wrenching, provided a sort of comfort. The brief ceremony offered a small way for April and me to care for our boy. Too late, too hollow, yes, I know, but something.

Even now, the ancient words below, though fraught with anguish, carry wisps of hope and comfort.

FROM THE BOOK OF COMMON PRAYER[7]
LITANY AT THE TIME OF DEATH

When possible, it is desirable that members of the family and friends come together to join in the Litany.

God the Father,
Have mercy on your servant.

God the Son,
Have mercy on your servant.

God the Holy Spirit,
Have mercy on your servant.

Holy Trinity, one God,
Have mercy on your servant.

From all evil, from all sin, from all tribulation,
Good Lord, deliver him.

By your holy Incarnation, by your Cross and Passion, by your precious Death and Burial,
Good Lord, deliver him.

By your glorious Resurrection and Ascension, and by the
Coming of the Holy Spirit,
Good Lord, deliver him.

We sinners beseech you to hear us, Lord Christ: That it may
please you to deliver the soul of your servant from the power
of evil, and from eternal death,
We beseech you to hear us, good Lord.

That it may please you mercifully to pardon all *his* sins,
We beseech you to hear us, good Lord.

That it may please you to grant *him* a place of refreshment and
everlasting blessedness,
We beseech you to hear us, good Lord.

That it may please you to give him joy and gladness in your
kingdom, with your saints in light,
We beseech you to hear us, good Lord.

Jesus, Lamb of God:
Have mercy on him.

Jesus, bearer of our sins:
Have mercy on him.

Jesus, redeemer of the world:
Give him *your peace.*

Lord, have mercy.
Christ, have mercy.
Lord, have mercy.

Officiant and People
Our Father, who art in heaven, hallowed be thy Name, thy kingdom come, thy will be done, on earth as it is in heaven. Give us this day our daily bread. And forgive us our trespasses, as we forgive those who trespass against us. And lead us not into temptation, but deliver us from evil.

The Officiant says this Collect
Let us pray.

Deliver your servant, *August Robert Hubbard,* O Sovereign Lord Christ, from all evil, and set *him* free from every bond; that *he* may rest with all your saints in the eternal habitations; where with the Father and the Holy Spirit you live and reign, one God, for ever and ever. *Amen.*

A Commendatory Prayer
Into your hands, O merciful Savior, we commend your servant *August Robert Hubbard.* Acknowledge, we humbly beseech you, a sheep of your own fold, a lamb of your own flock, a sinner of your own redeeming. Receive *him* into the arms of your mercy, into the blessed rest of everlasting peace, and into the glorious company of the saints in light. *Amen.* May *his* soul and the souls of all the departed, through the mercy of God, rest in peace. *Amen.*

An Obituary

M r. August "Auggie" Hubbard, age 19, of Orange City, passed away on October 23, 2020, in Orange City.

There will be a funeral service on Wednesday, October 28, at 6:00 PM, at Christ Chapel on the campus of Northwestern College in Orange City. The Rev. George Slanger will officiate. All those in attendance will be asked to use face coverings and abide by social distancing guidelines.

There will be a graveside service on Friday, October 30, at 2:00 PM, at the Edmore Cemetery near Edmore, North Dakota. The Oolman Funeral Home in Orange City is in charge of arrangements.

August Robert was born on December 22, 2000, in Grand Rapids, Michigan, to Robert and April (Blomquist) Hubbard. After moving to Iowa in 2002, Auggie attended Orange City Christian School and MOC-Floyd Valley High School in Orange City where he played in band as an All-State musician and participated in theatre and soccer. Growing up, he worked at the Orange City pool and at Fareway Grocery. He then attended Northwestern College in Orange City where he was currently a sophomore.

Auggie loved playing and listening to music. He masterfully played the tuba, bass guitar, and guitar. He participated in concert band, pep band, and theatre at Northwestern. He was an art-loving boy enchanted by big ideas and huge questions. He sought justice for the oppressed and always had a heart for underdogs. He advocated for his beliefs firmly, and would enthusiastically converse about them with anyone, always seeking greater knowledge. He deeply loved animals and spent much of his free time playing and cuddling with them, especially his feisty rat terrier/chihuahua mix, Medea.

Auggie's favorite thing to talk about recently was what his college major should be. A brilliant and passionate young man, he could not decide between history, music, psychology, political science, sociology, and theatre. He was just too interested in everything and wanted to find a calling where he could do the most good in the world. He was always concerned with helping people, whether it was through art, discovery, or institutional change.

Auggie became a confirmed member of the Church of the Savior in Orange City in 2019, after attending this church for many years with his family. This little Episcopal church has a tradition of discussing the sermons within the service, and Auggie was known and admired for his challenging and thoughtful questions and wise observations about theology and scripture.

Auggie is survived by his parents, Robert and April, of Orange City; brother, George Hubbard, of St. Paul, Minnesota; brother and sister-in-law, Charles Hubbard and Abbey Bos, of Des Moines; grandparents, George and Joanne Slanger, of Lakeville, Minnesota; grandmother, Violet Blomquist, of Edmore, North Dakota; uncles and aunts, Paul and Julie Saxton, Carol (Blomquist) and Danny Recuenco, Richard Blomquist; and cousins, Benjamin Saxton, Rachel Downing Saxton, Nicholas Saxton, Alexander Recuenco and Alison Recuenco.

He was preceded in death by his grandfathers, Robert Dean Hubbard and Charles Blomquist.

Memorials may be given to the Hubbard Family for future designation.

Dearest Friends and Family and Loved Ones

FACEBOOK POST: OCTOBER 23, 2020

Dearest Friends and Family and Loved Ones,

It seems that I must now share this post to avoid the hundreds of relived griefs that slowly come toward us. It is with deepest sadness that I share that our youngest son, Auggie Hubbard, took his own life last night after a long battle with depression.

Auggie was a sophomore in college. He loved playing the tuba, acting in theatre, and discussing philosophy, theology, history, and psychology. He was an art-loving boy enchanted by big ideas and huge questions. He sought justice for the oppressed and always had a deep heart for underdogs. In the days, weeks, and years to come, much more will need to be said about our wonderful son, brother, and grandson, Auggie Hubbard.

Unfortunately, Auggie struggled with the terrible, insidious disease of clinical depression. For most of the past four years, he tried every major form of treatment available with limited success. He did his best, he battled, and often experienced hope for the future. His favorite thing to talk about recently was what he would major in. A brilliant and passionate young man, he could not decide. He was just too interested in everything. He was in a good mood yesterday morning when I last saw him. The depression must have come upon him in the night and was just too much. The result is devastating and irreversible.

As a family, we pray and fervently hope that Auggie is finally at peace and that he now feels the joy, the eternal joy that his chemically starved brain deprived him from experiencing regularly these past four years. We also pray that his untimely death will not trigger more suffering among his classmates and friends. Rather, may Auggie's life and passing renew and remind us of what a precious gift this life is for us all.

As a family, we are unprepared even though we at times feared this horrible outcome. We are in shock and enduring unimaginable grief. Please pray for me, April, George, and Charlie, especially for April and George, both of whom share their own battles with clinical depression, a family monster. We need some time to gather ourselves to mourn, so please give us privacy for the short term. We'll let those around us know if we need anything other than your prayers; and we desperately need all of your prayers.

If you knew Auggie and if you choose to respond to this sad and terrible announcement, please share something positive and memorable about our wonderful son on this wall. We miss him so much and know that this wound will likely never truly heal, at least not in this lifetime. Our greatest comfort now resides in the future Kingdom and in the laughs and love we shared for nineteen years with this phenomenal, passionate, beautiful boy.

FACEBOOK POST: NOVEMBER 1, 2020

I asked Auggie not long ago if he had a favorite Bible verse. Because of his deep concern for the poor and the oppressed, and perhaps because of his own struggles with depression, he said that he liked the Beatitudes the most. I seem to recall that he said that Jesus's vision expressed in this passage is "how the world should work, Dad." For this reason, April and I chose the Beatitudes as the Scripture for Auggie's funeral last Wednesday. This morning, from a basement in Edmore, ND, I checked the Lectionary (https://episcopalchurch.org/lectionary/all-saints-day), the liturgical calendar for the Episcopal Church, and noticed that

Matthew 5:1–12 was the preassigned Gospel reading for today. In Auggie's memory, please do your best to live into these words this week and beyond.

MATTHEW 5:1–12 (NRSV)

When Jesus saw the crowds, he went up the mountain; and after he sat down, his disciples came to him. Then he began to speak, and taught them, saying: "Blessed are the poor in spirit, for theirs is the kingdom of heaven. Blessed are those who mourn, for they will be comforted. Blessed are the meek, for they will inherit the earth. Blessed are those who hunger and thirst for righteousness, for they will be filled. Blessed are the merciful, for they will receive mercy. Blessed are the pure in heart, for they will see God. Blessed are the peacemakers, for they will be called children of God. Blessed are those who are persecuted for righteousness' sake, for theirs is the kingdom of heaven. Blessed are you when people revile you and persecute you and utter all kinds of evil against you falsely on my account. Rejoice and be glad, for your reward is great in heaven, for in the same way they persecuted the prophets who were before you."

FACEBOOK POST: NOVEMBER 22, 2020

In light of recent events, it's probably time for an update from the Hubbards.

One month ago, we lost our beloved Auggie. Let me be clear: nothing about losing our talented, kind, smart, funny, justice-seeking son is okay. His long struggle with clinical depression was not fair, or positive, or justified. Losing him the way we did is an example of the evil grip that the Fall has upon our broken world. Auggie fought like hell for years, but the monster of depression took our wonderful son; we remain furious that we lost him, and we are racked with doubt and guilt. This is not the way things are supposed to be.

In our better moments, comfort can be found in the beautiful memories we shared with our wonderful boy. It hurts to remember, but we cling to the memories. We also find hope in the promise of the resurrection. From our shadowy vantage in this fallen world, we have experienced occasional glimpses of Auggie in a heavenly realm. We long for the moment when we can laugh, and argue, and hug, and join him again.

April and I have spent the past three weeks together at April's family farm in North Dakota. Through the constant waves of grief, time together was desperately needed, and we are grateful to family and our employers for their assistance and understanding. The only faculty member in her program, April recently returned to her job as the Theatre Director at Lake Region State College in nearby Devils Lake. After my colleagues graciously covered for me for weeks, I started teaching again online this past week. While difficult at times, we both appreciate the value of work and the distraction. After a few days of reuniting with our sons Charlie and George over Thanksgiving, I plan to return to Orange City to finish the semester in person at Northwestern.

Life goes on, of course, but we have no plans to return to normal. Our ability to function may improve, but we know that things will never be the same. This terrible wound will not and should not completely heal; our pain stems from a deep and righteous love for our son. As the song says, "The price of love is loss." As we try to move forward, we will pay this price; we will carry the terrible privilege of grief. We must mourn our son well. He's so worth it.

At such times, people don't know what to say. Well-meaning clichés abound. As April and I wade back into our daily lives, and yours, please know that we don't expect you to know what to say or do; we appreciate your prayers, your presence, and the countless gestures of love that have been expressed toward us this past month. No, we're not doing okay, but that's okay. We remain grateful for our friends and family and look forward to future fellowship, however clumsy or awkward.

To avoid clichés, I find myself turning to Shakespeare and Scripture. It seems that these powerful source texts come the closest to articulating our despair and disdain for the devastating events that have been allowed to occur as well as our fervent hope and trust in the light of eternity. For the former, King Lear shows me that Shakespeare knew what it was like to lose a child:

> "No, no, no life?
> Why should a dog, a horse, a rat have life,
> And thou no breath at all? Oh, thou'lt come no more,
> Never, never, never, never, never. —"
>
> (act 5, scene 3, lines 320–323)

As if in response, I also cling to Jesus's words to the thief on the cross:

> "Today you will be with me in paradise."
>
> (Luke 23:43 NIV)

FACEBOOK POST: JULY 1, 2021

People often ask swimmers what they think about when they swim. To be honest, maintaining good technique and keeping track of a set limit the amount of deep thinking one can do while swimming a workout. It's wrong to say that swimming stops me from thinking. It's more like a clearing of the brain, a settling down, a respite. There's something primordial about slipping through the water: weightless, clean, clear, quiet. We all spend our first nine months in water. There's probably a reason why Jesus, before starting his ministry, asked that crazy John fella to dunk him in the river Jordon.

I'm not sure why, but eight months after losing Auggie, swimming seems to be about the only place where grief doesn't attack.

It's there, of course, but its weapons of regret, longing, guilt, and anger seem to recede into the cool, churning water.

A professor's flexible summer work schedule (I recognize my privilege) combined with a few rainy days allowed me to swim many times in the month of June. My Apple Watch informed me today that I logged nineteen workouts for 55,150 yards (about thirty-one miles) in the past month. I swam more yards during my high school days, of course. But, old and slow and fat as I am now, I've never been more beholden to my time in the water.

FACEBOOK POST: JANUARY 22, 2022

Like many people, I find that I'm eating less meat than I used to, for a lot of reasons. But today, I found myself in Sioux Falls. For years, April and I drove Auggie up here for his weekly therapy appointments. Afterward, Auggie always wanted to go to Five Guys for an enormous, wonderful cheeseburger and a vanilla shake. Since I don't really drink, this is my toast: To Auggie!

FACEBOOK POST: SEPTEMBER 11, 2022

Nearly eighteen years ago, as a reward to our youngest son, Auggie, for finally getting potty trained, we brought a kitten into our home. Four-year-old Auggie, a *Star Wars* fanatic, named his jet-black kitty Mace Windo, after the only black Jedi at the time. As she grew into a cat, she chose Auggie as her human. She slept with him for nearly all his childhood. For most of her life, she showed ambivalence for the rest of the family and animosity toward me. I think there was a stretch of about five years where she wouldn't let me touch her. She was reclusive and cranky. Although she loved our first dog, Luke, she loathed his successors, Igor, Medea, and Cecil. They all soon learned not to mess with her. As she aged, she did soften some. After we lost Auggie, she gradually sought out affection from others, even me, but only on her eccentric terms.

Today, our very old cat, Macey, passed away.

Please don't lecture on theology of whether or not animals have souls. I choose to believe that she is entertaining our son in the Kingdom. She is surely happy to be with her human again, and Auggie must be so thrilled to cuddle with his Jedi kitty.

Through a Glass, Darkly

I was wrong about my wife.

For nearly seven years, two of our boys struggled with suicidal thoughts: George first, then Auggie. During this span of time, I occasionally offered up a coping mechanism that I remember hearing one of George's therapists use early on. The axiom goes something like this: "If you don't want to live for yourself right now, live for the people who love you." I intimately understand that this advice may not be effective for someone at the bottom of depression's evil pit, but it seemed to help at times. Auggie especially showed moments of intense empathy *after* he realized how distraught his suicidal ideation made his mom and me. "I'm worried about you," he would say. "You look sad? You need to be okay." I sometimes added an amendment to the axiom in conversations with Auggie. "If we lost you," I told him, "I would never recover, of course, but your mom . . . losing you would kill your mom. The depression you are feeling now will eventually pass. It will," I promised. "In the meantime, please, live for your mom, Auggie, because she will not survive without you." This tactic was not a disingenuous ploy; I completely believed it.

—

And in the first, devasting days following Auggie's death, my words appear prophetic. April has battled clinical depression, the family monster, for most of her life. Predictably, the grief of losing a son has pushed her to the edge. The term "inconsolable" falls short; we all fear for her safety. She finally arrives in Orange City the day after Auggie died, driven all nine hours from North Dakota by her seventy-eight-year-old mother; April is in no condition to take the wheel.

Her frightening moods vacillate between despair and rage. With bitter loathing, she blames herself for not being geographically near her son at the critical hour; she is certain that her presence in town would have prevented his death, and she will never forgive herself for not being here! With righteous fury, April also lashes out at God. After Auggie suffered for so long and came so far, she rages, "How could He be so cruel! I hate God. He's a bastard!" she yells when her well-intentioned mother tries to comfort her with religion. She tries not to lash out at me but fails. Understandably. After all, I am the one who promised to keep our college sophomore safe so that she could help the family financially and pursue a career by teaching theatre at a college near her hometown in North Dakota. I'm the one who said we could use the money. She never would have taken the damn job if I had not encouraged her!

This all may be true.

But most of all, more than God or me, April blames herself.

Over the next few days, my wife's body does its best to die. She cannot eat more than a bite at a time, and I do not think she sleeps more than an hour throughout the first hellish week. Like a Shakespearean tragedy, the local weather patterns mirror her volatile moods; an unseasonable October storm hits our town with two straight days of below-freezing temperatures joined by blustery winds and snow. Not once but twice, April leaves the house during this extended blow. Without telling anyone, she simply walks into the frigid winds alone. Using cars, Charlie and I search for her when we realize that she is gone. The first time, I track her fresh footprints in the snow and eventually find her on the golf course trail returning to our town after walking five miles straight down a country path. The second time, I intercept her on the connected trail outside of town as she rounds mile number three. Neither time does she wear a proper winter coat or gloves as the wind chill makes thirty degrees feel like five. Her rage and fury somehow keep the frostbite away.

As we plan Auggie's funeral, reserves kick in from somewhere outside of ourselves. Through constant tears, April manages to make a collage of photos for the memorial table. In a wretched irony, she builds this visual tribute to the life of our beautiful boy from the remnants of the panel of photos she constructed less than a year and a half ago for Auggie's high school graduation party. For the finishing touches, April sends me to the local pharmacy to print some recent photos for the display. As I stand in front of the Kodak Kiosk, I try and fail to connect my phone with the printer's Bluetooth so that I can print the photos.

As I toil beside the stupid photo printer, I cannot help but think of the dozens of times we stood in line in this humble small-town pharmacy to pick up antidepressant medication for Auggie, medications that, like me, utterly failed to protect him. I realize that, almost exactly two years ago, I jubilantly praised the Lord on my knees in this very pharmacy after receiving the precious phone call that Auggie made the All-State band. Another terrorizing question soon follows. How long will it be, I wonder, before I stand here again by myself to print photos for a collage for April's funeral display? For I truly do not believe my bride will survive this current loss. An uncontrollable wave of tears forces me to leave and walk around the block several times.

But by evening, something shifts. As the house fills with ex-tended family for the funeral tomorrow, I hang out my only suit-able suit on the curtain rod next to our washing machine. I cling to an irrational hope that the open air will cure the many wrinkles. Just yesterday, April yelled at me because the blue dress shirt I hung out to take to the funeral home for Auggie's viewing, the same shirt he wore for his high school graduation, had a stain that I failed to notice. So, when April appears around the corner, I assume to approve of the condition of my wrinkled suit, I flinch. But then I notice an expression on her face that resembles peace. She smiles at me—*smiles*—the first smile I recall seeing on any face for days. I wonder to myself, "What in the hell is going on in my wife's brain?"

If the word "inconsolable" falls short of describing the April of these hellish past few days, the word "rock" comes closer now. April comforts Charlie and George through the traumatic ritual of seeing their little brother's body at the family viewing later that evening. The next day, we cling to each other like desperate lovers throughout the heartrending yet surprisingly magnificent funeral service. George, Charlie, and Charlie's wife, Abbey, all offer musical tributes, heartfelt ballads for a little brother that set the scene for the eulogy offered by Auggie's elderly grandfather, a retired English professor, Episcopal priest, and living saint. No doubt, Auggie would have loved pondering over his grandpa George's eloquent sermon, which includes a poignant imagining of the afterlife that concludes Chekhov's play *Uncle Vanya*. As recited by Grandpa George, the longing speech concludes with the promise that beyond the grave "we will live a life of radiant joy and beauty. And we'll look back on this life of our unhappiness with tenderness."[8] April whispers in my ear, "That was so beautiful."

For at least an hour after the service, April stands beside me radiating inexplicably a solid grace. Against the plan, we break COVID protocols and personally hug hundreds of guests who have somehow found their way to Auggie's funeral and want to pay their respects to us. We will later notice that more than a thousand people streamed the service online. Our protective masks soaked with grateful tears, we genuinely appreciate and take strength from the massive, moving tribute to our boy. And I derive much-needed stamina from April's loving presence as we stand together outside the chapel at the end of the long, impromptu receiving line. How is she still standing through this grief and with no food or sleep? This beautiful woman still amazes me after almost three decades of marriage.

—

Later that night, with our heavy heads resting on our pillows, I learn the secret.

"I've seen him," she says. "I see him when I go on walks."

"What do you mean?" I ask, concerned.

"It didn't happen at first," she explains. "But the last couple of days, I've seen Auggie. He walks beside me. I've felt his presence."

In the flickering light of the muted bedroom television, I can clearly see April's face. She does not appear crazy as she speaks. Her eyes, while still puffy from the cathartic tears shed during the funeral, look almost tranquil, not wild and ominous like before.

"How does he look?" I ask.

"Handsome," she reveals. "He has a full reddish beard. He looks healthy too . . . a little older, but healthy and fit."

Auggie tried to grow a beard at various points during adolescence, but it never amounted to more than patchy and scraggly tufts of strawberry blond hair. I remember begging him to shave, fearing his attempt at facial hair might cause mean teenagers to make fun of him. He ignored my advice, of course, but eventually decided to shave after a high school jerk told him that he had "pubes on his face." Now he has a beautiful beard? A man's beard?

"I know this sounds crazy, but he tries to comfort me when I see him," April continues. "The first thing he said to me was, 'Mom, why are you so upset?'"

That sweet obliviousness sure sounds like Auggie.

"He said some things that you should know. He said he didn't mean to do it. He was in pain, but he didn't mean to die."

This explanation rings true. But even so, I cannot help but wonder if April's shattered brain subconsciously construed a comforting fantasy.

"What else did he say?" I ask.

"He said that I need to take care of you, and Charlie, and George. He told me that it is not our fault. He said that nobody should blame themselves."

My wife then shares something that does not sound like anything she would construct by herself, willingly or not, even in her depressed and fragile state. A committed Christian for all her life, April's faith recently took a slightly rebellious theological twist from mainstream evangelical Christianity. A few years ago, she read Rob Bell's *Love Wins* in a book club. This controversial best seller caused April to question the existence of hell. Like many so-called radicals of Rob Bell's ilk, April now prefers to believe that God's perfect love and forgiveness are powerful enough to save *all* sinners, even those who do not intentionally seek forgiveness or even know about Jesus. So, you can imagine my surprise when this Christian woman who does not believe in hell tells me the following words: "Auggie said not to let the devil win."

—

I wish that I could say that April's reports of divine intercessions put an end to her profound sorrow, but the truth is more complicated. In the months that follow, she still suffers the loss of our boy in frequent bursts of debilitating grief. Like me, she also still agonizes about what was left undone to save our son. During weaker moments, she even goes against Auggie's admonition and blames herself. April regularly sees a therapist, which helps, but I fear for my wife at times. People who feel as much as she does are never safe from the dangers of serious grief. But as the months wear on, new visits from our boy occasionally provide April respite from her doubt and misery.

"He says that he plays music all the time."

—

I do not know if Auggie really visits his mom. I hope he does. Christianity offers mixed messages on the topic. As an Episcopalian, I have acquired a sensitivity to ethereal phrases like "the cloud of witnesses" as mentioned in Hebrews 12. It could be true. And if I can see clearly enough to believe in an omnipotent and loving God and a resurrection, why not this extrabiblical tidbit? Still, when I have dared to share April's testimony with a few learned theologians, I've sensed their skepticism. Do they think that I think that Auggie is now a ghost? Doubt creeps in. Perhaps my wife's grief-addled brain invented these supernatural visitations as a survival mechanism. Who could blame her? But what if these loving visions are symptoms of a deeper mental illness?

The artist in me wants to embrace the poetry of April's otherworldly visions of our boy. This thought brings back a wonderful family memory. Like many families whose kids grew up in the 2000–2009 decade, the *Harry Potter* books provided important touchstones for our children's lives. An early reader, our oldest son, Charlie, devoured the books in elementary school. He loved to entertain his family by speaking in a British accent. April read the early books to Auggie and George until they could read the later ones for themselves. When the final film came out in 2011, Harry Potter had been a family friend for nearly a decade.

April and I had no choice but to take the boys to the local premiere of the final film, a midnight showing on a Thursday, school night be damned. Way past his bedtime, eleven-year-old Auggie predictably fell asleep on the couch as we waited to leave for the theater; we could not rouse him. We almost gave up, nearly canceling the crazy family outing, but we knew how upset Auggie would be if he missed out on the Orange City premiere. He may never have forgiven us. So, like terrible parents, we shook our youngest child until he finally revived. He woke up cranky but grateful to be included. The extra time it took us to bring Auggie into consciousness meant that we had to sit in the front row of the packed movie theater because all the other seats were taken.

This ridiculous proximity to the screen made the experience of the film more intense and visceral. Despite snobbishly pooh-poohing Rowling's books for years, I completely loved and surrendered to the final movie; I especially loved experiencing it front and center with my family.

One scene from the film ministers to me now as I contemplate April's visions of Auggie in a heavenly realm. Harry Potter fanatics can undoubtedly recite this scene from memory. After being struck down by Voldemort in battle, Harry finds himself in what appears to be a train station in heaven. His deceased teacher and mentor Dumbledore appears to him there. Dumbledore gives Harry some lovely advice in this tender little scene, including the resonating line: "Do not pity the dead, Harry. Pity the living. And above all, those who live without love." Before they part in the celestial train station, Harry and Dumbledore share the following exchange.

HARRY: Professor? Is this all real? Or is it just happen-
               ing inside my head?
DUMBLEDORE: Of course it's happening inside your head,
               Harry, but why on earth should that mean
               that it is not real?[9]

Like Dumbledore to Harry, maybe Auggie truly reaches through the cloud of witnesses to comfort his ailing mom. The boy I know certainly would do this if he could; he hated to see anyone suffer. I wish he visited me too, but this absence does not disprove April's experience. Perhaps my supremely sensitive wife possesses a unique spiritual gift, a wizardly perception that allows her to witness unseen and holy things. A line from *Hamlet* also comes to mind: "There are more things in heaven and earth, Horatio, than are dreamt of in your philosophy." Likewise, Saint Paul offers an echo of Shakespeare's celestial perception. In 1 Corinthians, Paul hints at a barely visible kingdom: "For now we see through a glass, darkly; but then face to face" (1 Cor. 13:12 KJV). Could it be that, "through a glass, darkly," April has eyes to see nourishing glimpses of our beautiful boy?

Auggie performed in a Shakespeare play two weeks before he died. He played the supporting role of Longaville in our college's production of *Love's Labour's Lost*. I directed. Because of COVID, we performed this autumn show in an outdoor park with the actors wearing transparent masks. Even under these weird conditions, I loved watching Auggie act; he truly gave his heart to it. Today, his final line in Shakespeare's lightest romantic comedy still echoes in my brain. It came after the love-struck Longaville learned the news that he and his fellow merry men must wait an entire year to see their newfound lovers again. Shortly before the lights went out for the final curtain call, Auggie earnestly stepped forward and recited the following line to his character's beloved: "I'll stay in patience, but the time is long."[10]

In the long months since, this vow of perseverance has become a nostalgic mantra for me. I cling to it. After losing Auggie, I admit that I struggle with unbelief. Every day. Why didn't God protect him? Will I really see my boy again? Or is my belief just a fairy tale? As I struggle, I try to remember that wiser people than me testify that faith is a decision. April's visions of our boy may not be provable, but I choose to believe. I like to think that Auggie found a way to save his mom. Unlike her, I must wait. "I'll stay in patience" to see my boy again, "but the time is long."

—

Three weeks after the funeral, April returns from a four-mile walk on the vast and bitter prairie of North Dakota in November. Her trek included a visit to Auggie's grave, a place she goes every day regardless of the weather. For over three weeks now, we have hunkered down together in her family's rural North Dakota farm, a much-needed respite, a space for mourning. Seeing my bundled-up bride return to the farmhouse after her long walk, I ask, "How was it?"

A glint of joy twinkles in April's large blues, the eyes Auggie inherited. She answers, "Auggie says that heaven is real. He says it's real, and it is now."

I am so glad that I was wrong about my wife.

In Gratitude for a Son
Stumbling through the ACTS Prayer

Over the last several years, I developed a pattern of praying as I walked to work. I usually prayed out loud, lowering my voice as people neared my path. I tried to be discreet, but I must have looked like a very odd person at times.

I generally used the ACTS format in my prayers: Adoration, Confession, Thanksgiving, and Supplication, perfectly timed for my sixteen-minute morning ramble. My prayer walks have been a blessing to me these past years as beloved family members battled clinical depression. These prayers tethered me to God through some difficult times.

But since we lost our beloved Auggie to suicide two months ago, I struggle to authentically find my way through all four stages of ACTS. Auggie's unfair disease and sinister death make "adoration" a particularly tough sell for my grieving brain. Intellectually, I am capable of adoring God, of marveling at creation, of rejoicing in the belief that my beautiful boy now resides in the warm embrace of a loving Savior. Emotionally, however, I'm not quite there. At my worst, I fear that I may be comforting myself with a fairy tale. And I resent God for allowing depression this dark, cruel victory.

My battling boy suffered so much for so long but had also come so far. Ironically, my wife and I found ourselves living in new hope the year before he died. In many ways, Auggie was doing better than he had since his depression's onset, and was often full of promise and passion for the future. Adoring the God who allowed my son to die seems false or disingenuous at times. But I once heard a sermon on the topic of balancing faith with doubt. The minister advised her congregation to "fake it till you make it." So, I'm wearily striving to "make it" to adoration. I often fall short.

Prayers of confession come easily from my dark heart brimming with regrets and guilt. I also easily fall into prayers of supplication. Begging God for relief and forgiveness does not require a lot of effort from the depths of despair. "I'm sorry" or "help me" play on a loop in my addled brain. I'm not sure if these prayers reach far beyond self-pity or selfishness, but I pray them compulsively anyway.

That leaves prayers of thanksgiving. A pattern emerges as I strive to express gratitude on my morning walk. First, I experience persistent thankfulness for the hundreds of acts of kindness directed toward my family since that terrible day two months ago: food, money, a GoFundMe campaign, letters, messages, cards, constant prayers, and more. People can be so kind, and I remain grateful, humbled, and overwhelmed. I see the face of Christ on my neighbors.

The second wave of thanksgiving prayers carries with it cathartic sorrow, for these prayers bring Auggie back to me. When I pass by a long-abandoned toy box in my house's front entryway, I see Auggie's smiling ten-year-old self clutch his favorite possession at the time—an NFL-sized football perpetually affixed to his hand through a solid year of elementary school.

As I step out the front door of my house, my muscle memory vicariously relives the thousands of passes I tossed his way in the city park across the street; he always craved one more chance at a diving catch. As I pass by the playground where Auggie practically lived in the summer months of his childhood, memories of his delightfully obsessive love for *Star Wars*, lightsabers, Yoda, and cosmic underdogs joyfully stab at me.

I am triggered by these visual cues, and the gates of gratitude open wider as I walk. I revel in memories of Auggie's capacity for deep joy when eating Ben and Jerry's ice cream, or watching a great film, or consuming a challenging book. I smile as I recall the way he would angrily thump the armrest of his seat in our minivan during long car trips when a character in a book made a poor decision. "No!" he would shout to no one in particular; he so wanted love and justice and a release from suffering for everyone, even the misguided fictional characters in the hundreds of books he passionately devoured.

I shake with laughter remembering the way toddler Auggie would loudly cackle when his brothers told silly jokes or when he witnessed slapstick humor in some random movie. His laugh cured everything. I bawl when reliving the sensation of how the house literally vibrated from the soulful, mournful, masterful bellows of Auggie playing his tuba.

I reminisce at Auggie's shockingly perceptive teenage insights into movies, theater, music, and philosophy. He loved art and ideas so much. I fondly summon up his challenging yet endearing questions about faith and religion that he bravely asked during sermon discussions at our little church; he lived his life as a seeker of truth.

As I walk and pray, dozens of memories flood my mind and invariably cause my voice to crack and my body to shake. Through the grief, I find myself so grateful for the privilege of knowing Auggie and for the opportunity to witness his sincere passion for life.

I've honestly never known anyone like him. He was, as one friend recently called him, a treasure. These thanksgivings may not be soothing or comfortable, but they persist as vital and holy. They resonate through the universe as primal celebrations of a beautiful life. And they are all I have of him now.

Auggie died two months ago tomorrow. Today, December 22, should have been his twentieth birthday. While angry and devastated by the loss, my family strives this day to celebrate his birth, the precious gift of his life. I am so grateful that I got to know Auggie Hubbard and be his dad.

Forever Young

After Auggie died, I could not bring myself to pick up my guitar. I tried once, thinking it might be good for me, but immediately felt nauseous after barely a strum. No great loss to the world of music, but a sincere loss to me. Previously a creative source of comfort and family unity, the guitar now carried the burden of failed prayers.

I first picked up a guitar in earnest at age eighteen. To get a job at a Christian summer camp in the Black Hills, I may have implied that I could play well enough to lead music for worship. In reality, I could barely eke out two tinny chords on the Ibanez I borrowed from my sister. The lie worked, and in the few months before my job at the camp began, I struggled to teach myself to properly play. Fortunately, a real guitar player joined our staff that summer. He graciously and competently led the music while I discreetly strummed by his side.

In this way, I learned camp-song classics such as "I Am the Resurrection," "Lord of the Dance," and "They Will Know We Are Christians by Our Love." By the end of that first summer, I played the borrowed instrument well enough to lead songs on my own. Soon thereafter, my parents gifted me a used Alvarez that I played in obsessive bursts. Once I mastered the requisite six chords, I pretentiously shifted into singer/songwriter mode, composing my share of heartfelt, sappy love songs to young women who have undoubtedly long forgotten our dopey puppy love. Despite my intense artistic dabbling, I never improved beyond the modest ability of an intermediate strummer.

My guitar flirtations persisted into fatherhood. When each boy was born, I lugged my battered Alvarez to the hospital. Secure and swaddled in April's exhausted arms, each newborn boy received my serenade of Bob Dylan's iconic masterpiece "Forever Young." With eyes alert and faces still pink from birth, Charlie, then George, then Auggie obliviously heard this strange new giant croon Dylan's music prayer for parenthood: an invocation for a love-filled life of joy and integrity. Of course, I know our newborn boys did not comprehend the meaning behind Dylan's musical prayer, but this sacred performance was not for their education. For me, playing "Forever Young" for my brand-new boys on my old guitar functioned as a liturgical blessing, a ritual of hope, a petition to providence.

Thankfully, our musical boys did not inherit my limited guitar-playing abilities. As they came of age, all three took advantage of the well-used Alvarez sitting in the house to teach themselves to play. With the advantage of YouTube tutorials and genuine musical ability, each son soon surpassed his father's fumbling skills. One by one by one, they graduated to their own guitars as birthday or Christmas presents. By the time we had three teenagers in the house, the sound of strumming often emanated from three different rooms at once.

Although he quickly superseded my skills on the guitar, Auggie, always the nonconformist, expanded upon his brothers' repertoire of stringed instruments; in addition to the guitar, he picked up the banjo and then the electric bass. He mastered the latter with dexterous ease and impressive, popping flair.

Introverts all, our boys usually played their instruments in the solitude of their rooms. But we sometimes persuaded them to play together on special occasions. Around campfires on camping trips or during visits to relatives in the Twin Cities, Charlie, George, and Auggie took turns picking songs to share; they loudly played each selection together, driven by delightful and supportive energy. These impromptu hootenannies were glorious.

In the fall of 2020, Charlie loaded his guitar into a moving van for Des Moines, where he started his first job; George packed up for his sophomore year of college in St. Paul; and Auggie, also a college sophomore, moved into a dorm eight blocks away—he was dedicated to giving the residential college experience one more try. With April in her second year of teaching theatre in North Dakota, I found myself at home alone. I took advantage of the solitude to pick up my nearly forty-year-old guitar. Through September and October, I obsessively struggled to learn another iconic melody written by the most-favorite son of Hibbing, Minnesota. Like "Forever Young," Bob Dylan's "Lord Protect My Child" and I share a history.

As every serious Dylan fan knows, "Lord Protect My Child" came into the world as an outtake on the 1983 album *Infidels* but later appeared in *Bootleg Series Volumes 1–3*.[11] Although I knew of it, I never carefully studied the song until depression descended on the lives of two of our children. Through this struggle, Dylan's musical plea for divine protection found me. The line about having his mother's eyes particularly resonated. Charlie, our only son not afflicted by depression, inherited my brown eye color. George and Auggie's large, piercing blue eyes look so much like their mom's that it seems like Dylan preemptively wrote a song commemorating the resemblance.

I spent hours on the living-room couch mastering Dylan's chord progressions and strumming patterns that early fall. Through repetition, I gradually adapted the song to fit my voice, dropping an octave for all the verses except the last one. Near the top of my limited vocal range, I belted out the final title refrain, "Lord, protect my child," an octave higher than I sang the previous verses. For me, this simple musical alteration made the classic line more emphatic and desperate, which is how I felt.

Again and again, I sang this song to myself and to my God. Our family had lived under the menacing threat of depression for so long. Putting good theology aside, I intuitively believed that singing Dylan's prayerful plea each morning and evening some-how provided prayer-warrior protection for our depressed children. Along with my ACTS prayers on my walk to work each morn-ing, singing "Lord Protect My Child" grew into a daily devotion. I remember picking up my guitar to pray Dylan's famous song on the morning and the evening of the final day of Auggie's life.

I cannot imagine ever summoning the will to play "Forever Young" or "Lord Protect My Child" again.

On Anniversaries

Five months have now passed—November, December, January, February, March—since that terrible day when I found my son. When the twenty-third day of each month arrives, so does a compounding, crippling weight. Auggie is no less gone on the twenty-second or twenty-fourth of each month. But for some sadistic reason, the grieving brain tortures itself even more on these dark anniversaries.

Two weeks before April 23, I feel an unexpected urge to pick up my long-dormant guitar. On Charlie's recommendation, I have recently been listening to Nick Cave, an Australian singer/songwriter who has been making critically acclaimed music for decades. I paid little attention except to note that Cave covered Dylan's apocalyptic ballad "Death Is Not the End." But Cave also recently lost a son, and the resulting devastation haunts his newer music. I entirely identify with Cave's despondent pain as reflected in desperate, angry ballads such as "Have Mercy on Me." And after listening to an older song called "Mercy Seat," I suddenly feel the urge to see if I can translate his poignant songs onto my guitar.

Although my body permits me to play now, I quickly discover that Cave's darker melodies contain too many tricky minor chords for me to master. The guitar app on my phone thoughtfully encourages me to try out an easier, more mainstream Cave song, a wistful, wordy ballad called "Into My Arms." For an hour or so,

I bastardize this beautiful lovesick song with my jerky rendition. Eventually, my stinging fingers, uncalloused from months of inaction, force me to stop.

The next day, I pick up my guitar again. Since my phone is charging in the other room, I attempt to remember the chords for "Into My Arms" without bothering to look up the tabs. As I strum from memory, I stumble onto a unique chord progression similar to Cave's melody, but different enough. I rarely hear new music in my head, but today a simple melody reveals itself. First, I hum an austere tune underscored by the derivative, gifted chords. Next, I start improvising words. When a line arrives that does not suck too much, I jot it down on a notepad that happens to sit on the living-room coffee table. Two hours later, I have a fully formed song that I never intended to write. This response to the muse consists of seven verses with one climactic bridge. The music and words come from my improvisational attempt to honestly answer a question that well-intended friends still ask me every day: "How are you doing today?"

I write my share of prose, but I do not consider myself a songwriter, poet, or singer. I'm even a worse guitar player. And yet, in my desperate solitude, I reluctantly feel a need to share my three-chord lament. But with whom? For reasons I do not fully understand, the idea of singing it to my family seems impossibly intimate. Over a FaceTime call, April flat out confirms this feeling, telling me that she cannot handle listening to it. In addition to violating COVID protocols, inviting someone over to my empty home to hear this brooding dirge strikes me as both pretentious and awkward.

For no audience but myself, I obsessively play the song over and over. Eventually, I make a recording on my phone so that I can study the song with more objectivity. Then April 23 arrives, the six-month anniversary of Auggie's death. After listening to my amateur recording, I impulsively post the link to Facebook. Within a few hours, nearly four hundred people listen to the YouTube link. A couple of friends make generous comments. A playwright I worked with years ago posts, "I just want to say that you have written a Johnny Cash–level song, sir." An English professor buddy astutely observes that the song reminds him of Nick Cave.

Despite the kind praise of friends, I do wonder if I made the right decision to publicly share the song. As I suspected, the darkness of the sentiment upsets and rattles some listeners, especially Christian friends who fear that I may be losing my faith. I may be. But as I further process my rationale, I realize my sincere motivation behind sharing the song: I pray that my honest expression of grief may somehow prove redemptive.

By artistically answering the question, "How are you doing today?" I hope listeners better understand the hellish impact of losing a son and take a step toward empathy. Or maybe my half-assed musical lament poorly played may one day assist someone enduring a similar grief, a pseudomusical way of letting others know that they are not alone. Anyway, for now, it is the best I can do. Maybe someday I'll write a play. Or a book.

The wound of losing Auggie will never fully heal. Anniversaries will continue to rip open the scar. I try to wear the open wound with a sense of gratitude and expectation. I'm so grateful for the nineteen years I got to be Auggie's dad. Now, as I cling to my Christian identity, I must somehow try to live within the hope of the resurrection.

In the Gospel of Mark, a terrified father with a sick son asks Jesus, "If you can do anything, take pity on us and help us." "If you can?" scolds Jesus. "Everything is possible for one who believes." The father replies, "I do believe; help me overcome my unbelief!" (Mark 9:22–24 NIV).

I prayed every single day for years that Jesus would also heal my sons, a prayer that went unanswered, at least unanswered in the way I hoped it would be answered. But now, during these long, yearning days without Auggie, the desperate father's words from Mark's Gospel continually find their way onto my lips: "Help me overcome my unbelief." I fervently pray more than ever for guidance, for hope, for the promise that I will see my boy again.

If I do, I suspect that Auggie will bluntly tell me what he thinks of my song and remind me what a terrible guitar player I am. But I also believe that our musical and empathetic child will tell me that he is happy I picked up the guitar again.

BECAUSE: A LAMENT

You ask me how I'm doing today
What in the hell am I supposed to say?
This crushed spirit is here to stay
Because our sweet boy is gone.

The food I eat seems devoid of spice.
The blood red sunset doesn't catch my eye.
The smell of coffee brewing brings little delight
Because our sweet boy is gone.

My wife and I hang on by a thread.
We cling to each other with tired arms of lead.
Our pleasure receptors, yeah, they're nearly dead
Because our sweet boy is gone.

I don't want to go to my job,
But I don't want to do anything; it's all one big slog.
Triggers find me there that make me sob
Because our sweet boy is gone.

If the Denver Broncos lose, I don't really care.
It hurts so much to watch them play without him
        sitting here.
At least when they lose, I'm already in despair
Because our sweet boy is gone.

I know that Jesus still loves me,
But I no longer trust Him to protect my family.
Guess I fell into some bad theology
Thinking that God would keep our boy safe at home
    with me.

    Because his wild golden hair shimmered like
        the sun
    Because the joy beneath his passion lifted
        everyone
    Because his unquenched thirst for justice could
        not be satisfied
    Because his long battle with depression should
        not be stigmatized.

Depression now has its hooks in me.
Sweet Jesus this can't be how it's supposed to be.
A less hollow man might embrace the mystery.
Me, I just want to hold my boy.

Lord, I just want to hold my boy.
Because I just want to hold my boy.

The Garage Rafters
A Dirge in Four Parts

PRELUDE: FEARS AND DEFENSIVE RATIONALIZATIONS

We lived in fear for years.

Prevention advocates often make pleas for more public awareness about the dangers of depression and suicide. I see the necessity of this important work and deeply empathize with families
who are genuinely surprised by the hideous reality of losing loved
ones. Nonetheless, pleas for increased awareness do not apply to
our situation. For years, we knew this *could* happen. We feared
suicide constantly. Alongside a dedicated community of mental
health professionals, we pursued every option we could to prevent
it: weekly cognitive behavioral therapy session, group therapy that
Auggie despised, dozens of medication changes, ECT (electroconvulsive therapy), in-patient care, constant check-ins, access to
suicide-prevention hotlines, and mental health contracts. Our son
did not die due to a lack of awareness that his depression was serious or dangerous. This blunt fact fails to ease the guilt and abiding
sensation that we failed him.

For long stretches, we did everything we could think of to keep
from leaving Auggie alone. At one point during his junior year of
high school, just before his longest hospital stay of nearly forty
days, we moved my mother in with us from Minnesota. Gripped
by severe depression, Auggie had stopped going to high school

altogether. We tried to make him go, but he refused. What was I supposed to do? Put my depressed seventeen-year-old son in a headlock and drag him to the car?

For nearly a month, my incredibly kind mom stayed with us so that April and I could make appearances at work. A gifted retired teacher, she patiently tried to help her grandson face the stack of papers sent home by the school, but Auggie would have none of it. Instead, she watched over him during the day and did her best to let him know that he was loved. But how long can you keep something like that up? You can't be home all the time, and you can't monitor an intelligent teenager every second of the day and night. You may think you can, but you can't.

So, for years, every time I entered our home, part of me feared. Once through the door, I immediately directed my voice up the stairway toward our depressed son's room and called out, "Auggie, are you home?" Most of the time, he answered with an irritated retort: "Yeah, I'm here." Each time when he did not respond my neck constricted, and I called out again. If no answer arrived from the second call, I slowly climbed the stairs to his room in terror, knocked on his door, waited a beat, and, with a deep breath, pushed my way in. Most of these times, he was not even there; either he hadn't come home yet, or he had left the house to jog around the nearby city golf course. Other times I found him stretched out on his bed in the deep, impenetrable, daytime sleep of major depression. A time or two, he had his headphones in, shutting out the world. Every single time I opened his door—until that final time—I exhaled in relief, my heart thumping like a jackhammer. Did I taste metal, or was that my imagination?

Our paranoia was justified. There were attempts and flirtations with attempts. Always honest and transparent, Auggie told us about them. Yes, he took the sharpest kitchen knife into his room and kept it in his desk drawer just in case. Yes, he put a belt around his neck and tried to trap it in the doorjamb, but the belt would not stay in place. Yes, he researched on the Internet which over-the-counter pills might do the deed if he swallowed enough of them. Yes, one time in a spontaneous wave of despair, he swallowed all the antidepressants left in the pill bottle—eleven pills in all.

With each new admission, we reacted with trips to the emergency room. Eventually, we skipped the middleman and drove straight to the behavioral care hospital in Sioux Falls, the only facility in the region that admitted teenagers. Several other preventative efforts also followed. The entire drawer of kitchen knives lived under our bed for nearly a year. I confiscated every belt in Auggie's room, or anything else, including his brand-new guitar strap, that might conceivably support his weight. We carefully hid or flushed all medications; we took Auggie's antidepressants away from him for periods of time and personally doled out each pill at the appointed hours. It all seems so foolish now, so hapless, so incomplete, so futile, but this was what we did, this was our world, this was how we lived.

The first four times Auggie confided in us his powerful suicidal thoughts prompted extended hospitalizations. Eventually his psychiatrist and psychologist, working as a team, deduced that such long-term stays in what was intended to be a short-term facility made Auggie appreciably worse. His doctors lamented that Auggie did not respond as they hoped to drug therapy, or cognitive behavioral therapy, or electroconvulsive therapy. Even the extreme option of hospitalization eventually fell into the same category of medical futility. What could be done for him? we begged.

Most of the time, he is safe, the doctors said. Locking him up in the hospital only robs him of his happier moments, of his coping mechanism of music, of his agency, of his hope of getting better, they said. We need to instead work, they said, really work on effective strategies to help Auggie ride out the darker volatile moods that periodically afflict him, especially at night, they said. He signed this contract stating he will ask for help the next time he is considering suicide, they said. Perhaps it's time for him to take more ownership of his care. He's an adult, after all. He may need more independence to take the next step in his healing, they said. He's lonely. How could he find more friends? He needs a bigger circle of care than just his family, they said. Yes, living in the dorms might be good for him, they said.

April and I did not know if these well-intentioned experts were correct, if they were wise, if they knew what the hell they were doing. We argued; we petitioned; we advocated; we did not always comply. Believe me, I know how this all sounds, and most days I can barely bear the guilt of our failed response. But we never stopped trying or worrying; we made no decisions complacently or without agony; our decisions were made in love and guided by hope and the advice of experts. This fact remains true even as hindsight tortures and taunts us with regret and self-loathing and shame. We never stopped trying. We never stopped worrying. But still, how could we let this happen? What in the hell were we thinking?

FIRST MOVEMENT: COLD COMFORT

During a low point a couple of years into Auggie's long battle with depression, a horrible and unshakable observation began haunting my thinking. Auggie talked a lot about wanting to kill himself during that time. Driving into our garage one day triggered the thought. From that day forward, each time I parked our car I secretly wondered what kept our suicidal son from hanging himself from the garage rafters. The rafters were twelve feet high and strong. Any chair or ladder could easily be kicked away; no waiting for pills to kick in or dealing with slippery doorjambs. I cannot stand the thought of how he would suffer, but it would be so simple. For months, for years, this terrible observation visited me. How could we prevent it? All he would need was ten minutes by himself and a length of rope.

I certainly did not mention this recurring horror to him or anyone, not even April, lest simply saying it out loud might make it happen. There was one close call, I remember, connected to our family's abiding love for watching movies together. After reading some good reviews, I foolishly invited Auggie to go to see the Lady Gaga remake of *A Star Is Born* with me. He said no, thank God. Unknown to me, a character in the film hangs themself from the rafters of a garage. When Auggie asked me later if the movie was any good, I discouraged him from seeing it. "Naw, it's sappy and poorly acted," I lied. "You'd hate it."

During his final year of life when Auggie's mental health seemed to improve, the garage rafters offered me a sick, ironic kind of solace. As I glanced up at the horizonal beams each time I parked the car, my tired, long-frightened brain rationalized what turned out to be a soothing lie. I told myself that Auggie's life must not be in as much danger as we had feared. If our son truly wanted to die, I surmised, surely he would have tested the garage rafters by now, after all these years.

This morbid deduction offered no cold comfort that dreadful day when Auggie took his life in his college dorm room during the fall semester of his sophomore year.

SECOND MOVEMENT: THE PRETENSE OF NORMALCY

After the funeral, we transported Auggie's body back to North Dakota to bury him next to his grandfather in the Blomquist family cemetery. With the generous permission of my employer, I stayed with April and her mother at the remnants of their family farm through the rest of October and all of November. The surviving Hubbards then spent the holidays together, Thanksgiving and Christmas, broken, diminished, yet linked more closely by tragedy. As the new year finally crawled toward its dark beginning, our family faced the inevitable yet unimaginable challenge of returning to normalcy, as if that were possible.

Eventually, April and I mutually agreed to try to keep our jobs, at least for now. This meant that I would stay in Iowa by myself in the empty house where we raised three boys together. April would continue living with her mother in North Dakota through the spring semester so that she could keep her position teaching theatre at the nearby college. Of course, Charlie resumed teaching high school math in Des Moines; George briefly stayed home in Iowa with me for a few blessed weeks until he moved back to St. Paul for his spring semester of college. As the bleakest days of a midwestern winter set in, I found myself home alone.

POSTLUDE: THE REPRISE

This is where I find myself now.

During these long winter nights, I fall into unhealthy patterns, I'm afraid. I distract myself during the day with work and at least two lifeline calls to April. By 6 p.m., I enter our empty house, eat a sad, unhealthy supper, and try to summon the strength to walk our dogs. If our German shepherd, Cecil, didn't require so much exercise, I might not move at all past 6 p.m. I don't want to do anything, or go anywhere, or see anyone, and a global pandemic conveniently cooperates with these reclusive impulses.

The dark winter evenings prove toughest to fill. I used to love to read, but I can't hold a thought or focus enough to complete a paragraph, much less a novel. Even the sentences I write at work trail into oblivion. Teaching proves a helpful distraction, but nearly every PowerPoint slide I make during this time contains enough glaring typos to embarrass a third grader. To even marginally function, I must ask someone to proof everything I write before publicly sharing it. The stress of losing a child has wreaked havoc on my cognitive abilities. How long will this go on? Is it permanent? For now, reading, or writing, or even listening to music requires more concentration than I can muster.

After walking the dogs, I typically retire to the basement to do the only thing that I can manage beyond staring at the walls: I stream depressing television. For reasons I do not fully understand, the gloomy distraction of Nordic noir speaks to me; it becomes a bit of an obsession. Gritty, bleak, and well-made Scandinavian shows like *Trapped*, *Bordertown*, and *Case* pass the time until after 1 a.m., when the kind escape of sleep finally appears possible.

Each evening, I shuffle toward the stairs that lead to the basement television. But first, I must walk directly past the outer door leading to our attached garage. The door has a large window at the top that permissively leaks the chills of winter into the stairwell. As I pass through the pocket of cooler air, I sometimes catch myself glancing through the window toward the garage rafters. Hours later, after finally achieving my fix of Scandinavian criminal deviance, I must climb back up the basement steps to let the dogs out and prepare for bed. But now, in my more tired and diminished state, I deliberately look away from the blackened window separating the garage from me. As the frigid air triggers goosebumps, I pick up my lumbering pace until I reach the neutrality of the kitchen.

I am doing my best to banish the new thought that now occurs from time to time when I pass by the garage, especially late at night. How simple it would be for me to open the outer door, to step into the winter air, to embrace the cool seclusion of the unheated, yet sealed, sanctuary, to make a place for myself on those strong rafters.

April and the Mare of Easttown

My evenings consuming dark Nordic TV shows eventually expands to include HBO's prestige lineup, and I land on the gritty and powerful limited series *Mare of Easttown*. I tell April about the show, and soon we are streaming it together. Although separated by hundreds of miles because of our jobs, sharing good art with my person lessens the distance and temporarily eases the stifling burden of our shared grief.

The titular Mare, played by Kate Winslet, has a lot to be angry about. Her ex-husband recently moved in next door with his younger fiancé. She verbally spars with her live-in mother on a daily basis. One of her oldest friends persistently and publicly attacks Mare for failing to solve a missing-person case. And her estranged daughter-in-law, a recovering drug addict, sues for custody of Mare's grandson.

Gradually, we learn the deeply buried root cause of Mare's anger: the suicide of her adult son, Kevin. A decade-old home video reveals a young Kevin frolicking on a beach with all the wonderful zeal of boyhood. Through clenched conversations with Mare's ex-husband, we learn about Kevin's preadolescent diagnosis with Tourette's syndrome and his later, increasingly unmanageable teenage descent into anxiety and depression. We then painfully flash back to an adult Kevin now a meth addict, frenetically berating his helpless mother for not giving him drug money. When later forced to seek therapy by her employer, Mare reluctantly reveals that both her father and her son killed themselves. We fear alongside Mare when her adorable grandson begins to show the same traits as his deceased father. Will this terrible cycle continue?

Also: When does anger, even righteous anger, destroy us? How do we overcome it?

Winslet is marvelously surly as the disheveled Mare, who perpetually sucks on a vape stick, drinks too much, and scowls at her unearned misfortune. She presses on, yes, but under a gloomy burden that most of us could never fully comprehend. And she has every right to be angry.

In his letter to the Ephesians, the apostle Paul warns, "'In your anger do not sin': Do not let the sun go down while you are still angry, and do not give the devil a foothold" (Eph. 4:26–27 NIV). Paul's difficult-to-follow advice accurately portrays anger as a legitimate, yet corrosive, force. *Mare of Easttown* shows these bleak truths in practice.

In a foreboding scene in the third episode, Mare sullenly drinks alone in a crowded bar. Her naive and newly assigned partner, Detective Colin Zabel, stumbles—literally—upon her. Awkward yet endearing, the inebriated Colin tries to connect with his antisocial partner, whom he may be a little sweet on. Forced to interact, Mare tells him, "I'm trying to drink away a bad thought." Before Colin mercifully leaves Mare alone, he innocently asks, "Hey, did I talk you out of that bad thought?" He did not, and the devil clearly found a foothold. Without providing specific spoilers, Mare commits a vengeful and illegal act so brazen that it threatens to destroy her career, her family, and more. With Paul's warning to Ephesians echoing in the background, Mare's unchecked anger devolves into a sinful and destructive hate.

And yet, hope may still abide somewhere for Mare. Despite her sulking anger, the fruit of love lingers within her. Through her dark moods, she still tries to be a good mom, a grandma, and a detective. Mare knows everyone in her economically distressed Philadelphia suburb. She works tirelessly to look after them. As a detective, she often bends rules to help the neglected and forsaken, showing kindness to a local drug addict and to a harmless prankster teenager. By the fifth episode, Mare begrudgingly attends mandated mental health therapy; by episode 6, she even shows signs to her therapist of wanting to lay down her weary burden.

The biblical antidote for hate is, of course, love. Once again, Paul provides an essential insight, this time in 1 Corinthians: "Love does not get angry. Love does not remember the suffering that comes from being hurt by someone" (1 Cor. 13:5 NLV). One of the Bible's greatest hits, this famous explanation of love offers counsel to Mare and to all of us who righteously struggle with anger.

A year after Auggie's death and two episodes into *Mare of Easttown*, April confided to me that she was jealous of Mare. Mare unashamedly displays her righteous anger to the oblivious world, something we both secretly fantasize doing during our weak moments.

Thankfully, my wife's admiration for Mare soon transformed into something else. Just a week later, she shared a new, wiser revelation that she experienced after reluctantly attending a Bible study organized by a persistent coworker. After mulling over Ephesians 4:31–32 (NIV) with her Bible study group, my wife realized the futility of fervently embracing what Paul would have called Mare's "bitterness, rage, and anger." "It's pretty clear that I'm going to have to forgive everyone, including myself and God," my wife admitted. "Anger doesn't help."

The Jersey

The mood is frantic this August morning as we struggle to make ready our Iowa home to move in three college women this fall. The plan is to sublease it for four months while I spend my academic sabbatical healing and trying to make art in the Bahamas. April will once again run the theatre program at Lake Region State College in Devils Lake, North Dakota. Not an ideal long-distance arrangement for this long-married couple, but we will make do for now. *My* master scheme for readying our house involved a light cleaning and some emptying of drawers in our boys' bedrooms to make room for the college students to stuff their stuff. Easy. But April, by far my better half, has other plans.

We don't often deep-clean our home, I confess, especially the boys' rooms. But to make the rooms habitable for young women, April bravely throws herself into the repulsive task of taming two decades worth of habitation by boys, then teenage boys, then young men. Respect for their privacy and embarrassment for our complacency prevent me from sharing more specific details concerning the worst of what was uncovered during this deep cleanse.

April begins with our eldest son's room. After completing college last May, boy number one moved out late last summer, married his exceptional soul mate, and rented an apartment in Des Moines, where he now teaches math at an underserved high school while his wife studies to become a veterinarian. We couldn't be happier for them.

After two days and three boxes moved to the basement, April ambitiously transitions her efforts to our middle son's dwelling. Spending his summer lifeguarding in St. Paul, son number two leaves his room typically overstuffed. Our fashionista, his cluttered space brims with the clothing of four fancy, metrosexual men and a shoe collection diverse enough to rival that of the spouse of a Filipino dictator. Three days later, I assist by carrying three stuffed suitcases to the basement and four boxes for donation, singlehandedly resupplying the higher-end men's fashion line at our friendly neighborhood Bibles for Missions thrift store.

Our youngest son's room, boy number three, remains untouched, as it has for some months now.

—

It is common, I understand, to leave a room like this alone, to keep it, to preserve it. April did make a small and courageous foray into the room to clean and organize it a bit last December, two months after Auggies's death. But most of his beloved possessions remain in this lonely, longing, and holy space. We usually keep the door closed. But a few times a week, we separately find our way in to grieve. I've taken to sitting on his bed, nostalgically readorned by April with Auggie's boyhood Scooby-Doo sheets and comforter, even though the room was last occupied by a nineteen-year-old college sophomore.

I usually weep while sitting on the bed, surrounded by artifacts of Auggie's obsessions: classic and battered video-game consoles; a long-untouched binder of NFL trading cards still wrapped in plastic; collections of dystopian sci-fi book series; and volumes of impenetrable philosophy, from Plato to Marx to Kant to Kierkegaard. Worn-out folders of tuba sheet-music, two bass guitars, their cases, their amps, their tangled cords, and a full-size electric keyboard further clutter the room with remnants of our talented boy's bottomless and desperate passion for music.

—

By now, days have passed since our two older boys' rooms were cleared; Auggie's room remains frozen, a time capsule of precious artifacts. Afraid to ask, I try to soften my delivery: "What do you think we should do about Auggie's room?"

"I'll take care of it," she says, averting her eyes to the floor.

"I can try to help."

"No. I'm doing it," she resolves. Although relieved, I am a little hurt to be left out of this terrible duty. But I can read my wife well enough to know to shut the hell up.

Nine months out from that dreadful day when our boy left us, unexpected moments of grief may occur less frequently, but they still happen. When they do, they snatch from us the deception of complacency, rip us from the belief that our lives will ever be the same. From our living-room sofa, I realize that April has been in Auggie's room for some hours now, and I don't hear her moving around up there. Concerned, I quietly climb the stairs to the second floor and peek to the left, through the threshold, to our youngest son's room. April sits with her back to me at the foot of Auggie's bed facing the open walk-in closet. A neatly ordered pile of clothing rests on the floor in front of her. She's going through his garments one by one.

The moment I happen to peer around the corner April's arms stretch forward at eye-level suspending a child-sized Denver Broncos football jersey in front of her, her fingers gently pinching the blue mesh fabric of its tiny shoulders. The jersey dangles in front of her, lifelike, almost as if someone is in it. From the upstairs hallway, I witness a mother holding this empty vessel, this proxy for her son, our son, as if in the moment before a loving embrace. An eight-year-old boy's jersey, loved by him and proudly worn by him longer than it reasonably fit. It covered and conformed to his torso, his beautiful little body. Within this tattered nylon shell, the remembered shape of Auggie's boyhood essence levitates between his mother's outstretched arms. How cruel to share his shape, how pitiless that this hollow shroud impersonates our fidgety, giggling boy, a joyful child once accurately described by an observant uncle as "criminally cute."

An instant from now, when my brave and mourning wife inevitably lowers the jersey, our beautiful boy's silhouette will be vanquished from the room. I can't witness this. I jerk back from the doorway and gently, silently crumble to a crouch on the stairs. Cradling my face in my hands, like Munch's silent scream, I curse fate and God and myself for allowing moments like these to be all we have of our unfinished son.

—

Two days later, April and I haul another load of donations to Bibles for Missions. Together, we carry the cardboard boxes through the rear loading door into the back room of the store and rest them on the large sorting table with all the other cast-off clothing from the generous town. When the kindly volunteer asks if we want a receipt, April's voice cracks, "No, thank you." My elegant wife then bolts for the door, and I follow, helpless.

When I catch her in the alley, she bends into my arms and laments, "I just gave away most of Auggie's clothing." I try to hold her, to comfort her. As we embrace, I think of the tattered Broncos jersey still sitting at home in the saved box, of her outstretched arms, of his little remembered body, and of how an oblivious college student subletter will have no knowledge of or appreciation for the magnificent child who bounced against those walls.

The Day before the Day

The day will not surprise me; I am prepared. For weeks, I observe it creep toward me on the calendar like an unwanted and painful medical procedure. I plan to commemorate the day by doing as little as possible, by resting, by refraining from work, a sabbath. I won't chip away at that faculty profile proposal I said I'd finish by next week of the University of the Bahamas work group, or the curriculum map, or more course descriptions. I won't write that unfinished film review, or another chapter in this book. Maybe I'll make the humid two-mile walk over the Sidney Poitier Bridge to Cabbage Beach and take a long swim in the ocean, but only if I feel up to it. Or maybe I'll simply lay the day away on the Murphy bed in my tiny efficiency apartment graciously provided by the University of the Bahamas (UB) as a landing spot for my semester-long academic sabbatical in Nassau. Maybe I will try to enjoy a good meal at a neighborhood restaurant, perhaps a place that Auggie would have liked.

The day before the day, today, falls on a Friday, a busy day in the rhythms of my strange sabbatical existence in the Bahamas. The introduction to theatre course that I coteach for UB meets from 10 a.m. until 1 p.m., although we mercifully try to wrap things up by 12:45 p.m. if possible. Nobody I encounter on this day, not my students or my colleagues, will know that my youngest son took his life three hundred sixty-*four* days ago. I intend to maintain my secret.

My contributions to the class go well, I hope. I mix a few group activities with PowerPoint slides and as many colorful theatre stories as I can muster. I appreciate the distraction and the joyful, inquisitive energy of the Bahamian students. After uncovering the material as best I can, and fielding all questions, I permit myself a glance at my watch. If I hustle, I may be able to make it to a movie matinee at the nearby Marathon Mall if I can successfully hop a jitney bus on Mackey Street outside the Dundas Centre for Performance Arts, where the course is taught. Like many theaters in struggling urban areas, the Galleria Cineplex has seen its better days. The management strangely does not post the showtimes anywhere on the Internet, but I know from experience that the first Friday matinee starts at 1 p.m. The moment I get to Mackey Street, I spot a jitney crawling toward me in the early afternoon traffic, and I'm off.

Twenty minutes later, I find myself standing inside the nearly empty mall scanning movie showtimes above the Galleria's ticket booth. What luck! The first showing of the new and acclaimed Wes Anderson film, *The French Dispatch*, starts in five minutes. Skipping lunch, I order popcorn and take my seat as the lights dim. I have watched three matinees here in the past three months during these cautious COVID times, and every time I have had the theater to myself. The Galleria Cineplex once again grants me a private screening.

As the genius of Wes Anderson's unique *mise-en-scène* unfolds, I catch myself wondering what Auggie would think of this strange, off-kilter, and visually lovely film about French art and culture. This happens a lot nowadays, but especially during movies. Even through the worst stretches of his depression, Auggie still loved to visit the silver screen; sometimes, it was the only activity we could get him to do. I often catch myself seeing films through his eyes. I am confident that he would adore *The French Dispatch*, devour it. Oh, how I wish he was sitting beside me now. He could never suppress laughter if the jokes were good and the spirit off-beat. With Auggie here, this empty theater would transform into a festive place. Without him, I struggle to maintain consciousness. A quirky, episodic film about a fictional French newspaper cannot compete with the weariness caused by a morning of teaching with no caffeine reinforcements or lunch. I manage to beat back sleep for most of the film.

The jitney ride back flies into the first burst of Nassau's three-hour rush hour. Schools have just let out, and the cars of parents retrieving their children clog the streets. At this rate, my bus ride home will take an hour or more. Every jitney in car-clogged Nassau returns downtown during each route, so I must first ride in the wrong direction into the urban heart of the city for a few plodding miles before the driver circles back toward my neighborhood. I could have walked the distance from the mall to my apartment in thirty minutes, but I love to ride the jitney.

I love the way Bahamians proclaim "Good day" when they first step up onto the crowded bus; I love observing the people: the broad-shouldered women in health-care uniforms on their way to or from their shifts; men in plaster-covered coveralls and steel-toed boots coming home from the construction projects that perpetually dot the island; middle-school children in their blue uniforms making their way; the extroverted homeless man who somehow rides without paying and who provides unsolicited color commentary on the surrounding dramas of each fresh city block; the rare white tourists, eyes wide and wondering if perhaps they made the wrong decision going over the hill on the #1 jitney.

I love the music the drivers play, an infusion of rake-and-scrape, rap, and gospel. I love watching them fearlessly maneuver the slender purple buses through the too-narrow passageways of seemingly impenetrable rush-hour congestion. I love passing by the one-story storefronts filled with independent women's fashion outlets presumedly named after their proprietors; the tiny hole-in-the-wall restaurants with handwritten signs advertising chicken souse or cracked conch or jerk; the numerous abandoned businesses, their fading, hurricane-damaged signs surviving as remnants of entrepreneurial dreams presently deteriorating into the muggy mire as all things do when left unattended in this tropic paradise.

Most of all, I love passing the plethora of vibrantly painted buildings that color the city of Nassau: bright yellows, oranges, purples, lavenders, pinks—the colors of Junkanoo that by comparison make the brown fields and gray cornstalks of an Iowa winter seem even more aloof, bland, and distant.

As I take in the luminous collage of urban, Caribbean life, I discover, to my surprise, that tears are streaming down my cheeks.

Dammit. Doesn't grief, that arrogant and demanding troll, realize that tomorrow is the anniversary of the day that Auggie left us, not today. Embarrassed, I wipe my leaking face with my COVID mask. Hopeful that no one on this noisy bus will notice the white guy crying, I throw my focus to the floor and try to discreetly ride out the ongoing rush.

As I gently quake in my seat, I hear the word "Mister." Looking up, I witness a middle-aged woman in dark green nursing scrubs reaching across the aisle. A folded pack of Kleenex rests in her outstretched hand.

"You take this now, dearie," she offers, her alto voice slightly muffled through the pink and red embroidery of her handmade mask. Her chestnut pupils elegantly contrast with the white of her tired eyes set against her bright brown brow; she peers at me with a mixture of kindness and understanding.

"Thank you," I mumble.

She says nothing more as I unwrap the cellophane and wipe my tears, but she holds me in her gaze for a time. She seems to know, to be attuned to the universal signifiers of loss. My tears subside as we ride together, this empathic stranger and me. We surf the purple jitney through the glorious web of humanity. I find strange comfort in her attentive silence and the oblivious, vibrant life all around us.

Epilogue

THE GHOST LIGHT'S GLOW

A ghost light is a single, naked electric lamp left burning on the stage in an unoccupied theater when it would otherwise be completely dark. Theater managers set out ghost lights for safety, so people passing through a dark theater won't accidentally fall into the orchestra pit or trip on a piece of scenery. Years ago, I took a blind shortcut through the black box theater where I work because the stage manager from the previous night's rehearsal must have forgotten to turn on the ghost light. I thought I'd be fine since I knew the space so well, but I walked straight into a sturdy and misplaced wooden chair. The blunt force trauma to my midsection, while not life threatening, sent me curled to the ground, incapacitated like a character in pratfall farce.

Without the ghost light, the darkness overwhelms. It offers just enough illumination to tentatively navigate the stage but not nearly enough light to rehearse, find a left-behind wallet or purse, or remind anyone of the magic that transpired earlier when that transcendent space was fully lit.

Without Auggie here, my world feels as if it is lit by a ghost light. Those of us who love him must now navigate through the dim shadows. I try to be grateful that I can see at all.

To make sense of this dim new world in which I find myself, I seek out the lived wisdom of others. Once my healing brain finally permitted me to read again, I ordered books on grief. Some were excellent. Favorites include Nicholas Wolterstorff's seminal *Lament for a Son*[12] (a book I read many years ago but returned to with lived urgency), Jerry Sittser's *A Grace Disguised*,[13] Tish Harrison Warren's *Prayer in the Night*,[14] and Chimamanda Ngozi Adichie's *Notes on Grief*.[15] In different ways, these meditations on loss and love, all beautifully crafted and rich in theological insight, helped me along this ongoing journey. I recommend them.

Sadly, many common Christian responses to grief fall short of helpfulness. Some are pedantic; some are lazy. Others deeply irritate me. A refrain that offends me the most comes when people of faith cavalierly claim to know and understand the will of God.

Perhaps I am simply not a good Calvinist, but phrases like "it's all part of God's plan" turn me away from faith. What kind of maniacal God would intentionally afflict Auggie with unrelenting major depression, let him suffer for years, and then, when parts of his life clearly and measurably improve, ruthlessly take him from us? Auggie should not have died. Period. His death was wrong, and terrible, and a symptom of how incomprehensibly broken our fallen world continues to be.

Years ago, long before untimely death intimately shook our family, April directed a Pulitzer Prize–winning play by David Lindsay-Abaire about the death of a child. In one scene from *Rabbit Hole*,[16] a character described as a "God freak" reflects, "I guess God needed another angel." The main character of the play, Becca, a flabbergasted mother who just lost her son in a senseless car accident, responds, "He's God! Why didn't he just make another angel? These people." I consider myself a "God freak," but I'm with Becca.

Bad things happen to good people every day; we become numb to the world's suffering until they happen to us. On a good day, maybe I get close to embracing the mystery of the problem of pain . . . on a good day. But please spare me attempts to make my son's death a positive outcome in God's divine plan. I believe losing my nineteen-year-old son to suicide illustrates the diabolical stranglehold that the Fall currently wields upon our desperately broken creation.

We all must live under the shadow of death. Rather than viewing God as the cause of death, I derive comfort from the image of Jesus weeping beside Auggie's body, as he did for Lazarus. Likewise, imagining our musical boy playing his tuba with the heavenly chorus brings some small comfort. But slogans like "it happened for a reason" or "it's all part of God's plan" offer no comfort.

To a lesser degree, I also resist a common thread found in Christian-influenced grief responses that disproportionately focus on positive outcomes resulting from terrible events. Paul's famous phrase from Romans 8:28 comes to mind: "And we know that in all things God works for the good" (NIV). Yes, the remarkable kindness and generosity shown to my family in the wake of Auggie's death continue to amaze and inspire me. Countless acts of goodness took place as a result of Auggie's death that otherwise would not have happened. An awareness of these grace-filled moments helped my family survive through a desperate and impossible time. So, yes, good does come from bad. My quibble turns on a matter of degree.

Without hesitation, I would gladly trade in *all* the good that resulted from Auggie's death; I would selfishly chuck it all to be with my boy again. I would give everything back and more, all the friendships, money, kindness, all of it, if doing so would somehow keep our son alive. Of course I would. This primal desire to turn back time certainly does not mean that I am not grateful for the many good things so lovingly given. But I would readily lay down my life and all I have for Auggie's survival if I could. I can't.

PHANTOM PAIN

Losing our son changed me.

This experience has figuratively disfigured me. I have used the term "wound," but the metaphor holds its limitations. Wounds make scars. Scars heal, even if they leave jagged and ugly marks. For me, the term "amputation" makes a far better metaphor. A piece of April and me is forever gone. As the months pass, I have incrementally learned to endure the loss well enough to get through most days, but the damage extends beyond a jagged and ugly scar. April and I have lost limbs. Phantom limb pain plagues us. Through self-care, therapy, and time, we have agonizingly figured out how to negotiate the world as emotional amputees, but we will never be the same.

I am also much more sensitive to violence and suffering than I used to be. If a movie or a TV show depicts death in some form, I must look away or even turn it off. Everyday events quickly evoke tears, like watching a mother on the nightly news talk about her child who died in a senseless shooting or learning about the victims of a tornado. Recently, a friendly dog on my normal walking route limped up to me on three legs. Once he got close, I noticed a deep gash on his right rear leg. I flat out fell apart. Even a comical scene in a farcical play in which one character pretends to strangle the other forced me to close my eyes and bury my chin in my chest. Such daily instances trigger a chain reaction of connected thoughts that move me through time and space. Before I can stop them, memories transport me back to that horrible dorm room where I found my son. I see it all again.

In the before times, I resisted the temptation to roll my eyes when my Generation Z students complained about being "triggered" by a play or book on the syllabus. "We can't censor life; we can't prepare for every negative event; c'mon, the play is called *Death of a Salesman*," I secretly thought. But in the glow of the ghost light, the pervasive pain percolating beneath the surface of the everyday *triggers* me constantly. Although I try to engage the world in healthy ways, I weirdly appreciate my increased sensitivity. For Auggie's sake, I hope it guides me to greater empathy and appropriate action toward those among us who suffer the most.

Relatedly, the persistent presence of profound grief has changed how I publicly confront suffering. In the first decade of the new century, Rachel Dratch played a *Saturday Night Live* character known as Debbie Downer, a flagrant narcissistic pessimist who, for comic effect, injected bad news or negative feelings into every social gathering. I did not want to be like Debbie. Since I was a boy, I innately feared inconveniencing people or making them uncomfortable. In what I understand is a common trait shared among adult children of alcoholics, I abhor conflict. As a result, I relentlessly guarded against oversharing or crashing the mood of social gatherings by saying unpleasant things.

No longer.

A few months after Auggie died, April set up a couple's appointment with a thanatologist in Sioux Falls. As I had to look up myself, thanatologists specialize in therapy for grieving the death of loved ones. This kind and competent gentleman helped me put away my persistent fear of being a Debbie Downer through the surprising use of animal metaphors. In what was clearly a speech he had given many times, he spent part of our session chronicling the behaviors of a turtle, an eagle, and a buffalo at the point in which they each encounter a storm. You probably see where this is going, but the turtle hides in its shell, the eagle soars above the storm, and the buffalo faces directly into the oncoming winds and walks straight forward. The thanatologist acknowledged that all three approaches work as survival mechanisms, but he claimed that the buffalo's approach was the healthiest.

As simplistic as this analogy may seem, its wisdom grabbed hold of me. We loved Auggie as much as a boy could be loved. Our approach to grieving him cannot be to hide or to try to get as far away as possible from that deep love. We need to love Auggie through grieving. Although walking into this storm causes discomfort, April and I intentionally try to turn into the wind. Sometimes we fail or fall short, but we try. If a memory of our boy occurs to me during a meal with extended family, I share it openly, with gratitude, and perhaps with a glinty tear, even though doing so predictably darkens the mood for a bit. Likewise, I often employ anecdotes gleaned from family experiences when teaching. Sometimes I plan them; other times, they pop into my head in response to a student comment or question. When an illustration involving Auggie occurs to me, I don't suppress it. For example: "In the First Folio, Shakespeare capitalized many words that he thought were important to the line of dialogue. My sweet son, Auggie, used to do the same thing in middle-school English class, even though he got marked down for it. He insisted on capitalizing important words." If sharing comments like this makes my students uncomfortable, they kindly carry on.

When guests visit our home, they encounter Auggie everywhere: several carefully selected photographs of all three brothers occupy prominent spaces on our many bookshelves; a framed self-portrait that Auggie drew in tenth-grade art class, his face etched with depression's despair, proudly hangs in our living room; his musical instruments decorate several corners of our home. Instead of burying these precious artifacts in the basement (the turtle) or storing them in the attic crawl space (the eagle), we lean into them as treasured, everyday reminders of our beautiful boy.

WHAT WOULD AUGGIE DO?

I became a Christian during a high point of late 1980s evangelicalism. Amy Grant topped the contemporary Christian music charts; every Christian youth event played a loop of Michael W. Smith's "Friends Are Friends Forever" on an old-school boom box; and teenagers my age wore wristbands embroidered with the letters *WWJD*. Today, in our observably more woke if cynical age, "What Would Jesus Do?" survives more as parody than as guidance. Even though the phrase admittedly represents an oversimplification of biblical exegesis, I remain curiously nostalgic for the term. Surely the bloviating iconoclasts who currently cheapen Christianity with anti-immigrant platitudes, hypermasculine perversions of Jesus's character, and prosperity-gospel blasphemies could potentially learn a lot if only they went back to square one and honestly tried to apply the red letters of the New Testament to their daily lives. Not that this is easy.

The medieval preacher Jacques de Vitry used the term "ex-emplum"[17] to describe a type of story told to illustrate a moral point. What lessons can be learned from my curation of stories from Auggie's life? From his death? From the life after? What, if anything, can we take forward as equipment for living? As I wrestle with these existential questions, the tongue-and-cheek phrase "What would *Auggie* do?" keeps pinging in my brain. I think Auggie would find this phrase hilarious. As I mourn his death. I am learning what his life has to teach me.

Stand up for the marginalized and side with the powerless. Like Jesus, Auggie always rooted for the underdog. I never heard him intentionally mock or mistreat anyone he thought were outsiders or who could not defend themselves. Like most families, our clan contains its share of colorful eccentrics who routinely engage in mildly irritating, if embarrassing, behaviors. Whenever one of these relatives came up in conversation, Auggie resolutely refused all gossip. "You shouldn't talk about —— that way," he would rebuke. "You wouldn't say that if he was sitting right here, would you?" To a fault, he loathed inequality and injustice in all forms. True, this predisposition led to frustrating infatuations such as his deep dive into Reddit communism, but Auggie's love for the neglected other never waned. It was sincere and real and important. He desperately wanted a better, more equal world.

Practice extravagant kindness. Throughout his life, our awkward boy struggled to fit in. Unlike his brothers, he never found a best friend, never had a girlfriend. This longing for companionship beyond his family was the reason that he moved into his college dorm. He so wanted to find a place to belong.

Auggie's depression surely skewed and increased his self-perception as an outcast. People in his life did show kindness to him, both in high school and in college. Based on the memorial service organized by the college shortly after his death, an outside observer would conclude that Auggie Hubbard was a popular fellow. But the kind and appreciated words said after his death do not change the reality that Auggie's many apparent admirers rarely sought him out in his secluded dorm room. Tragically, Auggie did not have the social skills to seamlessly enter other people's lives. During his darker moments, he could not feel the love around him. He needed extra help. For anyone who might read this sentence, I make the following, desperate plea: *practice extravagant kindness to the outsiders and marginalized souls among us.* For the love of my son, please do so even if this love is not invited. Especially if it is not invited. Knocking on that closed dorm-room door honors Auggie.

Be passionate. Martin Luther is famously attributed the phrase "Love God and sin boldly." The story of Auggie's life mirrors this radical approach to zealous living. His passionate nature formed an essential characteristic of his being, from zestfully hugging his day-care providers good-bye, to turning blue with rage, to joining the chorus of angels at a strange church, to dueling imaginary Siths in Windmill Park, to shattering Accelerated Reader records, to diving for footballs, to obsessively practicing his tuba. Auggie boldly modeled passionate living.

Keep learning. Auggie perpetually scoured the world for new insights into the meaning of life. He craved knowledge and pursued wisdom. While still in high school, he even used his limited Christmas money to purchase philosophy books. His love of learning made choosing a major in college almost impossible. A single academic discipline could not contain his many interests. He needed to know and understand our world. Never stop learning.

Love art and support artists. First through bedtime stories, then through novels, then through movies, then through music, then through theatre, Auggie loved art. The pursuit of truth through beauty impacted him more than most. If the art was good—and he had excellent taste—a catharsis followed. He lived it. He loved and suffered the world through art. He rejoiced in it. Art comforted Auggie. I had hoped that art might save him; it did not, but art did sustain him through many of his darker moments. A Vonnegut classic inspired euphoria. Likewise, the sonorous memories of his mourning tuba and angry, popping bass guitar still echo in our empty house.

Live in joy. This final edict synthesizes this entire list. For me, it is also the hardest to follow. Prior to the onslaught of his five-year battle with depression, I never met a person with more capacity for joy than Auggie. Admittedly, I often struggle to feel joy in a world without my boy. But this I know: nothing would make Auggie sadder than knowing that his death caused so much sadness. Throughout his depression, he constantly worried about his mom and me. He often used the phrase "you need to be okay" when he realized how worried and shaken his depression made us. Perhaps he lived as long as he did because of a desire to keep us from suffering.

—

Now that he is gone, I fervently pray that Auggie finally knows eternal joy. Out of love for Auggie, I try to live in the reflection of this joy. At the very least, I fake it till I make it. For him, I strive with gladness to help the marginalized; I love God by sinning boldly; I continue learning new things; I keep making art.

Although this grief does not end, I am blessed with a brain not predisposed to clinical depression. Unlike Auggie, the family monster graciously skipped me; my depression remains situational. I therefore intentionally and fervently dedicate the remainder of my life to the pursuit of joy. Because that is what Auggie would do, if he could.

In closing, I return to a phrase from Shakespeare also referenced earlier. In his words—also the final line that my favorite undeclared theatre major ever said on stage: "I'll stay in patience; but the time is long."

Acknowledgments

S everal kind people helped usher this book along. I shared an early draft with trusted friends who provided valuable, honest, and gracious feedback. In particular, I'd like to thank my Northwestern College colleague and church brother Mike Kugler for his thoughtful coffee conversation. Jerry Sittser and Nick Wolterstorff, two luminary writers whom I barely know in real life but whose related works profoundly influenced this book, graciously offered encouragement on an early draft. Indeed, Nick suggested I send it to Eerdmans.

I also must thank those who endured the proofing and editing process. My then-student work-study assistant, the brilliant Karisa Meier, proofed multiple drafts, fixing dozens of hapless typos and suggesting several helpful edits. My parents, George and Joanne Slanger, provided early feedback as well. My mom, being a mom, sent her draft copy to a librarian friend, Jane La Plante. Thank you, Jane, for your careful edits. Finally, I could not be more grateful to Lisa Ann Cockrel and, later, Jenny Hoffman at Eerdmans for seeing value in this book and for making it so much better.

Most of all, I'd like to thank my family. *Scenes with My Son* was not easy for them to read, but they pulse through every page like a heartbeat. Charlie and George, please know that your love keeps me alive. To April, my love, my partner, my best friend, thank you.

Notes

1. Maggie O'Farrell, *Hamnet: A Novel of the Plague* (New York: Knopf, 2021).

2. *The Soul of Wit: G. K. Chesterton on William Shakespeare*, edited and introduced by Dale Ahlquist (Newburyport, UK: Dover, 2013), 58.

3. *The Poetics of Aristotle*, chap. 6, trans. S. H. Butcher, Project Gutenberg, 1999, http://www.gutenberg.org/etext/1974.

4. Jay Roach, dir., *Trumbo* ([Madrid]: Aurum Producciones, 2016).

5. Brian Yorkey and Tom Kitt, *Next to Normal* (New York: Theatre Communications Group, 2010).

6. Car Seat Headrest, "Drunk Drivers/Killer Whales," *Teens of Denial*, Matador Records, 2016.

7. Episcopal Church, *The Book of Common Prayer, and Administration of the Sacraments; and Other Rites and Ceremonies of the Church, according to the Use of the Protestant Episcopal Church in the United States of America: Together with the Psalter, or Psalms of David* (Oxford: Oxford University Press, 1979).

8. David Mamet and Anton Pavlovich Chekhov, *Uncle Vanya* (New York: Samuel French, 1988).

9. David Yates, Steven Kloves, Daniel Radcliffe, Rupert Grint, Emma Watson, Helena Bonham Carter, Robbie Coltrane, et al., *Harry Potter and the Deathly Hallows. Part 1. Part 2* (Burbank, CA: Warner Home Video, 2012).

10. William Shakespeare, *Love's Labour's Lost*, act 5, scene 2.

11. Bob Dylan, *The Bootleg Series Volumes 1–3* (2017).

12. Nicholas Wolterstorff, *Lament for a Son* (Grand Rapids: Eerdmans, 1987).

13. Gerald Lawson Sittser, *A Grace Disguised: How the Soul Grows through Loss* (Grand Rapids: Zondervan, 1995).

14. Tish Harrison Warren, *Prayer in the Night: For Those Who Work or Watch or Weep* (Downers Grove, IL: InterVarsity, 2021).

15. Chimamanda Ngozi Adichie, *Notes on Grief* (New York: Knopf, 2021).

16. David Lindsay-Abaire, *Rabbit Hole* (New York: Theatre Communications Group, 2006).

17. *The Exempla or Illustrative Stories from the Sermones Vulgares of Jacques de Vitry* (n.p: Published by D. Nutt, 1890).